NEW COLORFUL NINJA FOODI

POSSIBLECOOKER
COOKBOOK FOR BEGINNERS

Super Easy, Healthy and Flavorful PossibleCooker Recipes to Steam, Bake, Sear and Slow Cook Every Day| Enhanced with Color Pictures

Cynthia Green

I penned this cookbook with a singular goal in mind: to share the joy, convenience, and boundless potential that the Ninja Foodi Possible Cooker PRO brings to the kitchen. This cookbook is not just a collection of recipes; it's an invitation to join me on an exhilarating culinary expedition. It's an opportunity to maximize your kitchen space, unleash your culinary creativity, and savor the immense satisfaction that comes from cooking an array of dishes with a single, versatile appliance.

So, if you're ready to elevate your culinary skills, simplify your kitchen setup, and embark on a journey of culinary discovery, this book is your gateway. The Ninja Foodi Possible Cooker PRO is your key to unlocking a world of flavors, techniques, and delicious meals. I invite you to embrace the possibilities, immerse yourself in the world of cooking, and relish the experience of creating extraordinary dishes with ease.

Join me in celebrating the Ninja Foodi Possible Cooker PRO and the art of culinary exploration. Let this cookbook be your guide, and may your culinary adventures be as exciting and fulfilling as mine have been. Get ready to embark on a flavorful journey—one that promises endless culinary delights and unforgettable meals. Happy cooking, and may your kitchen always be filled with the aroma of success!

TABLE OF
CONTENT

INTRODUCTION

Hello, I'm Cynthia Green. Life often throws us into unfamiliar territories, and me, that meant leaving the comfort of my family's home to venture out on own. As I settled into my new life, I realized that one of the biggest challen I faced was mastering the art of cooking beyond the basics.

My kitchen journey began with the trusty air fryer, a lifesaver for prepa quick, simple, and delicious meals. But deep down, I craved more. I yea to explore the world of cooking with a wider range of techniques and ingr ents. There was just one problem: my kitchen space was limited, and I cou possibly clutter it with a multitude of single-purpose gadgets like slow cool woks, and more.

Then, one day, I stumbled upon the Ninja Foodi Possible Cooker PRO, it was nothing short of a revelation. This incredible kitchen marvel offer plethora of functions, including slow cooking, searing, baking, braising, st ing, and even sous vide. It was a versatile powerhouse that replaced a w arsenal of single-purpose tools, instantly expanding the boundaries o kitchen.

Using the Ninja Foodi Possible Cooker PRO was like unlocking a trea chest of culinary possibilities. Its user-friendly design made it a breeze t erate, and every meal became an exciting adventure. I dove into the wo sautéing, perfected the art of slow-cooking hearty soups, and delighted i rich flavors of slow-cooked stews. My culinary horizons expanded, and n etary life was enriched in ways I couldn't have imagined.

It was this incredible experience that led me to create this cookbook. I these pages, you'll find over 100 meticulously crafted recipes, spanning mouthwatering breakfast creations to delectable desserts, hearty main co to soul-warming stews, and exquisite meat dishes that will dazzle your buds. Each recipe is accompanied by detailed step-by-step instruction vibrant, captivating images to guide you on your culinary journey.

INTRODUCTION

Hello, I'm Cynthia Green. Life often throws us into unfamiliar territories, and for me, that meant leaving the comfort of my family's home to venture out on my own. As I settled into my new life, I realized that one of the biggest challenges I faced was mastering the art of cooking beyond the basics.

My kitchen journey began with the trusty air fryer, a lifesaver for preparing quick, simple, and delicious meals. But deep down, I craved more. I yearned to explore the world of cooking with a wider range of techniques and ingredients. There was just one problem: my kitchen space was limited, and I couldn't possibly clutter it with a multitude of single-purpose gadgets like slow cookers, woks, and more.

Then, one day, I stumbled upon the Ninja Foodi Possible Cooker PRO, and it was nothing short of a revelation. This incredible kitchen marvel offered a plethora of functions, including slow cooking, searing, baking, braising, steaming, and even sous vide. It was a versatile powerhouse that replaced a whole arsenal of single-purpose tools, instantly expanding the boundaries of my kitchen.

Using the Ninja Foodi Possible Cooker PRO was like unlocking a treasure chest of culinary possibilities. Its user-friendly design made it a breeze to operate, and every meal became an exciting adventure. I dove into the world of sautéing, perfected the art of slow-cooking hearty soups, and delighted in the rich flavors of slow-cooked stews. My culinary horizons expanded, and my dietary life was enriched in ways I couldn't have imagined.

It was this incredible experience that led me to create this cookbook. Inside these pages, you'll find over 100 meticulously crafted recipes, spanning from mouthwatering breakfast creations to delectable desserts, hearty main courses to soul-warming stews, and exquisite meat dishes that will dazzle your taste buds. Each recipe is accompanied by detailed step-by-step instructions and vibrant, captivating images to guide you on your culinary journey.

I penned this cookbook with a singular goal in mind: to share the joy, convenience, and boundless potential that the Ninja Foodi Possible Cooker PRO brings to the kitchen. This cookbook is not just a collection of recipes; it's an invitation to join me on an exhilarating culinary expedition. It's an opportunity to maximize your kitchen space, unleash your culinary creativity, and savor the immense satisfaction that comes from cooking an array of dishes with a single, versatile appliance.

So, if you're ready to elevate your culinary skills, simplify your kitchen setup, and embark on a journey of culinary discovery, this book is your gateway. The Ninja Foodi Possible Cooker PRO is your key to unlocking a world of flavors, techniques, and delicious meals. I invite you to embrace the possibilities, immerse yourself in the world of cooking, and relish the experience of creating extraordinary dishes with ease.

Join me in celebrating the Ninja Foodi Possible Cooker PRO and the art of culinary exploration. Let this cookbook be your guide, and may your culinary adventures be as exciting and fulfilling as mine have been. Get ready to embark on a flavorful journey—one that promises endless culinary delights and unforgettable meals. Happy cooking, and may your kitchen always be filled with the aroma of success!

CHAPTER 1
BREAKFAST

Vanilla Cinnamon Pumpkin Pudding

SERVES: 8

PREP TIME: 15 minutes
COOK TIME: 6 hours

¼ cup melted butter, divided
4 eggs
2½ cups canned pumpkin purée
2 cups coconut milk
½ cup granulated erythritol
2 ounces (57 g) protein powder
1 tbsp. pure vanilla extract
1 cup almond flour
1 tsp. baking powder
¼ tsp. ground nutmeg
1 tsp. ground cinnamon
Pinch ground cloves

1. Lightly grease the inside of the pot with 1 tbsp. butter.
2. Add the remaining butter, coconut milk, pumpkin, eggs and vanilla in a large bowl, and whisk together until well blended.
3. Place the erythritol, almond flour, baking powder, protein powder, nutmeg, cinnamon and cloves in a small bowl, stir them together.
4. Combine the dry ingredients with the wet ingredients. Pour the mixture into the pot, then cover with the lid.
5. Turn dial to SLOW COOK, set temperature to LOW, and set time to 6 hours. Press START/STOP to begin cooking.
6. When cooking is complete, serve immediately.

Creamy Mashed Potatoes

SERVES: 10

PREP TIME: 15 minutes
COOK TIME: 3 hours

1 tbsp. extra-virgin olive oil
4 cups mashed potato flakes
1½ cups 2% milk
1 pkg. (8 oz., 227 g) cream cheese, softened
½ cup butter, cubed
½ cup sour cream
3¾ cups boiling water
1 tsp. garlic salt
¼ tsp. pepper
Minced fresh parsley, optional

1. Lightly grease the inside of the pot with olive oil.
2. Add the milk, butter, cream cheese, sour cream and boiling water into the greased pot and whisk together until smooth.
3. Add the garlic salt, potato flakes, and pepper and stir well. Then cover with the lid.
4. Turn dial to SLOW COOK, set temperature to LOW, and set time to 3 hours. Press START/STOP to begin cooking, until heated through.
5. When cooking is complete, sprinkle with parsley if desired and serve hot.

Slow Cooked Spiced Pear Oatmeal

SERVES: 1

PREP TIME: 5 minutes
COOK TIME: 8 hours

3 cups unsweetened almond milk or water
¾ cup steel-cut oats
1 ripe pear, cored, peeled, and diced
¼ tsp. cinnamon
⅛ tsp. ground ginger
⅛ tsp. ground cardamom
⅛ tsp. ground nutmeg
⅛ tsp. sea salt

1. Place the ginger, cardamom, oats, nutmeg, cinnamon and salt in the pot, and stir to combine well. Add the almond milk and pear, stir well. Cover with the lid.
2. Turn dial to SLOW COOK, set temperature to LOW, and set time to 8 hours. Press START/STOP to begin cooking.
3. When cooking is complete, serve immediately.

Chicken and Broccoli Quiche

SERVES: 8

PREP TIME: 15 minutes
COOK TIME: 12 minutes

½ tbsp. olive oil
1 frozen ready-made pie crust
1 egg
¼ cup boiled broccoli, chopped
¼ cup cooked chicken, chopped
⅓ cup cheddar cheese, grated
3 tbsps. whipping cream
Salt and black pepper, to taste

1. Lightly grease the pot with olive oil.
2. Whisk egg with whipping cream, cheese, salt and black pepper in a small bowl.
3. Arrange the pie crust in the pot. Press in the bottom and sides gently and pour the egg mixture over pie crust.
4. Top evenly with chicken and broccoli, then cover with the lid.
5. Turn dial to BAKE, set temperature to 390°F, set time to 12 minutes, and select START/STOP to continue cooking.
6. When cooking is complete, remove the lid and serve warm.

Cherry Tomato Frittata

SERVES: 2

PREP TIME: 10 minutes
COOK TIME: 10 minutes

2 tbsps. olive oil, divided
3 eggs
4 cherry tomatoes, halved
½ of Italian sausage
1 tbsp. Parmesan cheese, shredded
1 tsp. fresh parsley, chopped
Salt and black pepper, to taste

1. Turn dial to SEAR/SAUTÉ, set temperature to HI, and select START/STOP to begin preheating. Allow the unit to preheat for 5 minutes.
2. Meanwhile, whisk together eggs with Parmesan cheese, 1 tbsp. olive oil, parsley, salt and black pepper and beat until combined.
3. When preheating is complete, heat 1 tbsp. olive oil in the pot. Cook the sausage uncovered for 2 minutes, stirring occasionally.
4. Add the tomatoes to the pot and cook for 2-3 minutes.
5. Drizzle the egg mixture over sausage and tomatoes in the pot. Stir to combine, then cover with the lid.
6. Turn dial to BAKE, set temperature to 360°F, set time to 5 minutes, and select START/STOP to continue cooking.
7. When cooking is complete, remove the lid and serve warm.

Spinach Casserole

SERVES: 4

PREP TIME: 10 minutes
COOK TIME: 20 minutes

Cooking spray
1 (13.5-ounce / 383-g) can spinach, drained and squeezed
2 large eggs, beaten
1 cup cottage cheese
¼ cup crumbled feta cheese
2 tbsps. all-purpose flour
2 tbsps. butter, melted
1 clove garlic, minced, or more to taste
1 ½ tsps. onion powder
⅛ tsp. ground nutmeg

1. Lightly grease the pot with cooking spray.
2. Combine the spinach, eggs, cottage cheese, feta cheese, flour, butter, garlic, onion powder, and nutmeg in a medium bowl. Stir until all the ingredients are well incorporated.
3. Pour the mixture the pot, then cover with the lid.
4. Turn dial to BAKE, set temperature to 375°F, set time to 20 minutes, and select START/STOP to continue cooking, until the center is set.
5. When cooking is complete, remove the lid and serve warm.

Classic Huevos Rancheros

PREP TIME: 10 minutes COOK TIME: 3 hours	1 tbsp. extra-virgin olive oil 10 eggs 1 cup shredded Monterey Jack Cheese, divided 1 cup heavy (whipping) cream 1 cup prepared or homemade salsa 1 scallion, green and white parts, chopped 1 jalapeño pepper, chopped 1 tbsp. chopped cilantro, for garnish 1 avocado, chopped, for garnish ½ tsp. chili powder ½ tsp. salt

1. Lightly grease the inside of the pot with olive oil.
2. In a large bowl, add the heavy cream, eggs, salsa, ½ cup of the cheese, jalapeño, scallion, chili powder and salt and whisk together. Pour the mixture into the pot and sprinkle the remaining ½ cup of cheese on the top. Then cover with the lid.
3. Turn dial to SLOW COOK, set temperature to LOW, and set time to 3 hours. Press START/STOP to begin cooking, until the eggs are firm.
4. When cooking is complete, slightly cool the eggs, then cut into wedges and garnish with avocado and cilantro. Serve warm.

Vanilla Quinoa and Fruit Breakfast

PREP TIME: 5 minutes COOK TIME: 8 hours	2 cups fresh fruit 3 cups water ¾ cup quinoa 1 tsp. vanilla extract ⅛ tsp. sea salt 2 tbsps. toasted pecans, for garnish

1. Place the fruit, quinoa, and salt in the pot. Stir in the water and vanilla extract and combine thoroughly, then cover with the lid.
2. Turn dial to SLOW COOK, set temperature to LOW, and set time to 8 hours. Press START/STOP to begin cooking.
3. When cooking is complete, garnish with a sprinkle of the toasted pecans and serve immediately.

Simple Breakfast Casserole

PREP TIME: 10 minutes COOK TIME: 22-23 minutes	½ tbsp. olive oil 3 eggs 3 red potatoes, diced 2 turkey sausage patties ¼ cup cheddar cheese 1 tbsp. milk

1. Turn dial to SEAR/SAUTÉ, set temperature to HI, and select START/STOP to begin preheating. Allow the unit to preheat for 5 minutes.
2. Meanwhile, whisk the eggs with milk in a bowl.
3. When preheating is complete, heat the oil in the pot and cook the potatoes uncovered for 7-8 minutes, stirring occasionally.
4. Add the sausage to the pot and pour the egg mixture on top. Sprinkle with cheddar cheese. Then cover with the lid.
5. Turn dial to BAKE, set temperature to 350°F, set time to 15 minutes, and select START/STOP to continue cooking.
6. When cooking is complete, remove the lid and serve hot.

Ritzy Vegetable Frittata

PREP TIME: 15 minutes COOK TIME: 21 minutes	½ tbsp. olive oil 4 eggs 1 zucchini, sliced ½ bunch asparagus, sliced ½ cup mushrooms, sliced ½ cup spinach, shredded ½ cup red onion, sliced	¼ bunch chives, minced, for garnish ¼ cup milk 5 tbsps. feta cheese, crumbled 4 tbsps. Cheddar cheese, grated Sea salt and ground black pepper, to taste

1. Turn dial to SEAR/SAUTÉ, set temperature to HI, and select START/STOP to begin preheating. Allow the unit to preheat for 5 minutes.
2. Meanwhile, in a small bowl, mix the eggs, milk, salt and pepper.
3. When preheating is complete, place the olive oil and vegetables in the pot and cook uncovered for 5 minutes, stirring occasionally.
4. Once cooked, pour in the egg mixture over the vegetables. Top with the feta and grated Cheddar. Cover with the lid.
5. Turn dial to BAKE, set temperature to 320°F, set time to 15 minutes, and select START/STOP to continue cooking.
6. When cooking is complete, remove the lid and let the frittata cool for 5 minutes.
7. Top with the minced chives and serve.

Lush Vegetable Omelet

PREP TIME: 10 minutes COOK TIME: 13 minutes	2 tsps. canola oil 4 eggs, whisked 1 green bell pepper, seeded and chopped 1 red bell pepper, seeded and chopped 1 white onion, finely chopped ½ cup baby spinach leaves, roughly chopped ½ cup Halloumi cheese, shaved 3 tbsps. plain milk 1 tsp. melted butter Kosher salt and freshly ground black pepper, to taste

1. Lightly grease the pot with canola oil.
2. Put the remaining ingredients in the pot. Stir to combine well, then cover with the lid.
3. Turn dial to BAKE, set temperature to 350°F, set time to 13 minutes, and select START/STOP to continue cooking.
4. When cooking is complete, remove the lid and serve warm.

Breakfast Sausage Frittata

PREP TIME: 15 minutes COOK TIME: 20 minutes	cooking spray 4 eggs, lightly beaten ¼ pound breakfast sausage, fully cooked and crumbled ½ cup Monterey Jack cheese, shredded 1 green onion, chopped 2 tbsps. red bell pepper, diced 1 pinch cayenne pepper

1. Lightly spray the pot with cooking spray.
2. Whisk together eggs with sausage, bell pepper, green onion, cheese and cayenne in a bowl.
3. Transfer the egg mixture into the pot, then cover with the lid.
4. Turn dial to BAKE, set temperature to 365°F, set time to 20 minutes, and select START/STOP to continue cooking.
5. When cooking is complete, remove the lid and serve warm.

CHAPTER 2
VEGETABLES

Sesame Asparagus with Soy Sauce

SERVES: 4

PREP TIME: 5 minutes
COOK TIME: 7 minutes

1 tbsp. vegetable oil
2 pounds (907 g) asparagus, trimmed and cut diagonally into 2-inch-long pieces
2 large garlic cloves, coarsely chopped
2 tbsps. light soy sauce
2 tbsps. sesame oil
1 tbsp. toasted sesame seeds
1 tsp. sugar
Kosher salt

1. Turn dial to SEAR/SAUTÉ, set temperature to HI, and press START/STOP to begin preheating. Allow the unit to preheat for 5 minutes.
2. In a small bowl, stir the light soy and sugar together, until the sugar dissolves. Set aside.
3. When preheating is complete, add the vegetable oil to the pot and coat the bottom well. Place the garlic and sauté until fragrant, about 10 seconds.
4. Add the asparagus to the pot and cook until crisp-tender, about 4 minutes, seasoning with a small pinch of salt.
5. Pour the soy sauce mixture and stir to coat the asparagus evenly, cooking for about 1 minute more.
6. When cooking is complete, press START/STOP to end cooking. Drizzle the sesame oil over the asparagus and garnish with the sesame seeds. Serve warm.

Spicy Napa Cabbage

SERVES: 4

PREP TIME: 6 minutes
COOK TIME: 7 minutes

2 tbsps. vegetable oil
1 head napa cabbage, shredded
3 or 4 dried chili peppers
1 tbsp. light soy sauce
2 peeled fresh ginger slices, each about the size of a quarter
2 garlic cloves, sliced
½ tbsp. black vinegar
Kosher salt
Freshly ground black pepper

1. Turn dial to SEAR/SAUTÉ, set temperature to HI, and press START/STOP to begin preheating. Allow the unit to preheat for 5 minutes.
2. When preheating is complete, add the oil to the pot and coat the bottom well.
3. Season the oil with the chilies. Let the chilies sizzle in the oil for about 15 seconds. Put the ginger slices and a pinch of salt. Let the ginger sizzle in the oil for about 30 seconds, swirling gently. Stir the garlic in and stir-fry lightly to flavor the oil, about 10 seconds. Do not let the garlic turn brown or burn.
4. Add the cabbage to the pot and sauté until it wilts and turns bright green, about 4 minutes.
5. Pour the light soy and black vinegar and season with a pinch of salt and pepper to taste. Toss to coat for another 20 to 30 seconds.
6. When cooking is complete, press START/STOP to end cooking. Discard the ginger. Serve warm.

Garlic Eggplant

PREP TIME: 10 minutes
COOK TIME: 8 minutes

3 tbsps. peanut oil
2 Chinese or Japanese eggplants, cut into bite-size pieces
4 garlic cloves, minced
1 scallion, chopped
1 tsp. cornstarch
SAUCE:
2 tbsps. soy sauce
1½ tbsps. Chinese black vinegar or apple cider vinegar
1½ tsps. brown sugar
2 tsps. chili bean paste
1 tsp. dark soy sauce

1. Make the sauce by mixing together the vinegar, soy sauce, dark soy sauce, brown sugar and chili bean paste in a small bowl. Set it aside.
2. Turn dial to SEAR/SAUTÉ, set temperature to HI, and press START/STOP to begin preheating. Allow the unit to preheat for 5 minutes.
3. Meanwhile, coat the eggplant with a light layer of cornstarch.
4. When preheating is complete, heat the peanut oil in the pot. Sauté the eggplants, uncovered, for 3-4 minutes, until cooked almost all the way through.
5. Add the garlic to the pot and cook until fragrant.
6. Pour the sauce to the pot, stir-frying until all the ingredients are mixed.
7. When cooking is complete, press START/STOP to end cooking. Garnish with the chopped scallion and serve hot.

Honey Brussels Sprouts

PREP TIME: 10 minutes
COOK TIME: 10 minutes

¼ cup honey-flavored butter
1 pound (454 g) Brussels sprouts, grated
½ cup chopped onion
2 tbsps. white cooking wine
Salt and ground black pepper to taste

1. Turn dial to SEAR/SAUTÉ, set temperature to HI, and press START/STOP to begin preheating. Allow the unit to preheat for 5 minutes.
2. When preheating is complete, melt the honey-flavored butter in the pot. Sauté the onion, uncovered, for 5 minutes, stirring occasionally.
3. Add the Brussels sprouts, salt and pepper to the pot and cook for about 5 minutes, stirring occasionally.
4. Press START/STOP to end cooking and pour in the wine and toss to coat well. Serve warm.

Honey Drizzled Carrots

SERVES: 4

PREP TIME: 5 minutes
COOK TIME: 50 minutes

1 tbsp. olive oil
1 pound baby carrots
4 tbsps. vegan butter
3 tbsps. honey
1 tbsp. agave nectar
¼ tsp. ground cardamom
¼ tsp. kosher salt

1. Before getting started, add 12 cups of room-temperature water to the pot.
2. Cover with the lid and turn dial to SOUS VIDE, set temperature to 180°F and set time to 45 minutes. Press START/STOP to begin preheating.
3. Add the carrots, honey, whole butter, kosher salt, and cardamom to a resealable bag.
4. When preheating is complete and "ADD FOOD" will show on the display.
5. Open the lid. Place the bag in water and seal it using the water displacement method. Close the lid.
6. When cooking is complete, remove the bag with carrots from the pot.
7. Strain the glaze by passing through a fine mesh. Set aside.
8. Pour off any remaining water and pat the pot dry with a paper towel. Turn dial to SEAR/SAUTÉ, set temperature to HI, and press START/STOP to begin preheating. Allow the unit to preheat for 5 minutes.
9. When preheating is complete, heat 1 tbsp. oil in the pot. Place the carrots in the pot and cook for 2-3 minutes, until the carrots are tender.
10. Pour any excess glaze over the carrots. Serve with a little bit of seasonings.

Sous Vide Balsamic Onions

SERVES: 2

PREP TIME: 3 minutes
COOK TIME: 2 hours

2 medium white onions, sliced julienne
3 tbsps. olive oil, divided
1 tbsp. balsamic vinegar
2 tbsps. brown sugar
Salt and pepper to taste

1. Before getting started, add 12 cups of room-temperature water to the pot.
2. Cover with the lid and turn dial to SOUS VIDE, set temperature to 185°F and set time to 2 hours. Press START/STOP to begin preheating.
3. Mix the onions with the remaining ingredients, except 1 tbsp. olive oil in a Sous Vide bag.
4. When preheating is complete and "ADD FOOD" will show on the display.
5. Open the lid. Place the bag in water and seal it using the water displacement method. Close the lid.
6. When cooking is complete, remove the bag with onions from the pot.
7. Pour off any remaining water and pat the pot dry with a paper towel. Turn dial to SEAR/SAUTÉ, set temperature to HI, and press START/STOP to begin preheating. Allow the unit to preheat for 5 minutes.
8. When preheating is complete, heat 1 tbsp. olive oil with cooking spray. Place the onions in the pot and cook until the onions are tender.
9. Serve warm.

Garlic Eggs and Bok Choy

SERVES: 3

PREP TIME: 5 minutes
COOK TIME: 5 minutes

2 tbsps. cooking oil
6 eggs, beaten
1 cup chopped bok choy
¼ cup hoisin sauce
3 garlic cloves, crushed and chopped
3 scallions, cut into ½-inch pieces
2 tbsps. soy sauce
2 tbsps. rice wine

1. Turn dial to SEAR/SAUTÉ, set temperature to HI, and press START/STOP to begin preheating. Allow the unit to preheat for 5 minutes.
2. When preheating is complete, heat the cooking oil in the pot until it shimmers. Sauté the garlic, uncovered, for 10 to 15 seconds or until lightly browned, stirring occasionally.
3. Add the eggs and rice wine to the pot and stir-fry until the eggs are firm but still moist.
4. Place the scallions and cook for 30 seconds.
5. Then add the bok choy and cook for 1 minute, stirring occasionally.
6. In a small bowl, combine the soy sauce and hoisin sauce. Drizzle over the scrambled eggs.
7. Press START/STOP to end cooking. Serve warm.

Daikon Radishes

SERVES: 4

PREP TIME: 10 minutes
COOK TIME: 30 minutes

1 tbsp. olive oil
½ cup white winger vinegar
1 large size Daikon radish, trimmed and sliced up
3 tbsps. beet sugar
2 tsps. kosher salt

1. Before getting started, add 12 cups of room-temperature water to the pot.
2. Cover with the lid and turn dial to SOUS VIDE, set temperature to 180°F and set time to 30 minutes. Press START/STOP to begin preheating.
3. Mix the radish, vinegar, salt, and beet sugar in a large bowl. Transfer to a Sous-vide zip bag.
4. When preheating is complete and "ADD FOOD" will show on the display.
5. Open the lid. Place the bag in water and seal it using the water displacement method. Close the lid.
6. When cooking is complete, remove the bag with radish from the pot.
7. Pour off any remaining water and pat the pot dry with a paper towel. Turn dial to SEAR/SAUTÉ, set temperature to HI, and press START/STOP to begin preheating. Allow the unit to preheat for 5 minutes.
8. When preheating is complete, heat some olive oil in the pot. Place the radish in the pot and cook until the radish is tender.
9. Serve warm.

Cooked Fingerling Potatoes

PREP TIME: 10 minutes
COOK TIME: 47 minutes

8 ounces fingerling potatoes
Salt, and pepper to taste
1 tbsp. unsalted vegan butter
1 sprig rosemary

1. Before getting started, add 12 cups of room-temperature water to the pot.
2. Cover with the lid and turn dial to SOUS VIDE, set temperature to 190°F and set time to 45 minutes. Press START/STOP to begin preheating.
3. Season the potatoes with salt and pepper and transfer them to a resealable zip bag.
4. When preheating is complete and "ADD FOOD" will show on the display.
5. Open the lid. Place the bag in water and seal it using the water displacement method. Close the lid.
6. When cooking is complete, remove the bag with potatoes from the pot. Cut the potatoes in half (lengthwise).
7. Pour off any remaining water and pat the pot dry with a paper towel. Turn dial to SEAR/SAUTÉ, set temperature to HI, and press START/STOP to begin preheating. Allow the unit to preheat for 5 minutes.
8. When preheating is complete, melt the butter in the pot. Place the rosemary and potatoes in the pot and cook for 2 minutes, until the potatoes are crispy.
9. Season with a bit of salt if needed. Enjoy!

Apple and Sweet Potatoes

PREP TIME: 15 minutes
COOK TIME: 7 hours

3 tbsps. butter, melted
2 lbs. (about 6 medium, 907 g) sweet potatoes or yams
1½ cups applesauce
⅔ cup brown sugar
1 tsp. cinnamon
chopped nuts, optional

1. Peel the sweet potatoes, then cut into cubes or slices. Place the sweet potatoes in the pot.
2. Add the butter, applesauce, brown sugar and cinnamon into a small bowl, mix well. Spoon over the potatoes, then cover with the lid.
3. Turn dial to SLOW COOK, set temperature to LOW, and set time to 7 hours. Press START/STOP to begin cooking, until the potatoes are tender.
4. When cooking is complete, spoon the sweet potatoes into a serving dish and top with the sauce. Sprinkle with nuts, if you wish.

Pineapple Sweet Yams

SERVES: 10

PREP TIME: 5 minutes COOK TIME: 3 hours	cooking spray 2 tbsps. dark brown sugar 40-oz. (1.1 kg) can unsweetened yams, drained 10-oz. (283 g) can unsweetened crushed pineapple, drained

1. Lightly spray the inside of the pot with cooking spray.
2. In a medium bowl, add the brown sugar and crushed pineapples and combine well.
3. Place the yams and the sugar mixed pineapples in the pot, then cover with the lid.
4. Turn dial to SLOW COOK, set temperature to LOW, and set time to 3 hours. Press START/STOP to begin cooking, until heated through.
5. When cooking is complete, serve hot.

Slow Vegetable Roast

SERVES: 8

PREP TIME: 10 minutes COOK TIME: 4 hours	6 medium white potatoes, cut into 1-inch cubes 6 large carrots, cut into ½-inch rounds 3 sweet onions, cut into ½-inch cubes 12 ounces (340 g) green beans (fresh or frozen) 8 ounces (227 g) mushrooms, sliced 4 cups vegetable broth 1 tsp. onion powder 1 tsp. garlic powder 1 tsp, freshly ground black pepper

1. Add all the ingredients in the pot. Stir together so the spices are well distributed. Then cover with the lid.
2. Turn dial to SLOW COOK, set temperature to HI, and set time to 4 hours. Press START/STOP to begin cooking.
3. When cooking is complete, remove the lid and stir well before serving.

Savory Tex-Mex Kale with Garlic

SERVES: 8

PREP TIME: 20 minutes COOK TIME: 4 hours	4 large tomatoes, seeded and chopped 4 bunches kale, washed, stemmed, and cut into large pieces 2 onions, chopped 8 garlic cloves, minced 2 jalapeño peppers, minced 1 tbsp. chili powder ½ tsp. salt ⅛ tsp. freshly ground black pepper

1. Place the kale, onion, garlic, jalapeno and tomatoes in the pot and mix well.
2. Add the chili powder, salt and pepper into the pot, gently stir to combine, and cover the lid.
3. Turn dial to SLOW COOK, set temperature to LOW, and set time to 4 hours. Press START/STOP to begin cooking, until the kale is soft.
4. When cooking is complete, remove the lid and serve immediately.

CHAPTER 3
GRAIN AND RICE

Vegetable Egg Fried Rice

PREP TIME: 10 minutes
COOK TIME: 3-5 minutes

2 tbsps. cooking oil
4 large eggs, beaten
1 medium onion, diced
1 medium carrot, julienned
1 red bell pepper, diced
2 cups cold, cooked rice
1 cup frozen peas, thawed
4 scallions, cut into ½-inch pieces
2 garlic cloves, crushed and chopped
1 tbsp. soy sauce
1 tbsp. ginger, crushed and chopped
1 tsp. sesame oil
½ tsp. kosher salt

1. Turn dial to SEAR/SAUTÉ, set temperature to HI, and press START/STOP to begin preheating. Allow the unit to preheat for 5 minutes.
2. When preheating is complete, heat the cooking oil in the pot until it shimmers. Sauté the garlic, ginger, salt and eggs, uncovered, for about 1 minute, stirring occasionally.
3. Add the onion, carrot and bell pepper to the pot and cook for 1 minute, stirring occasionally.
4. Toss in the peas, rice, sesame oil and soy sauce and stir-fry for 1 minute.
5. When cooking is complete, press START/STOP to end cooking. Garnish with the scallions and serve hot.

Shrimp Fried Rice with Peas

PREP TIME: 15 minutes
COOK TIME: 3-4 minutes

2 tbsps. cooking oil
2 cups cold, cooked rice
2 large eggs, beaten
½ pound (227 g) medium shrimp, peeled, deveined, and halved lengthwise
1 cup frozen peas, thawed
1 medium onion, diced
4 scallions, cut into ½-inch pieces
2 garlic cloves, crushed and chopped
1 tbsp. ginger, crushed and chopped
1 tbsp. soy sauce
1 tsp. sesame oil
½ tsp. kosher salt

1. Turn dial to SEAR/SAUTÉ, set temperature to HI, and press START/STOP to begin preheating. Allow the unit to preheat for 5 minutes.
2. When preheating is complete, heat the cooking oil in the pot until it shimmers. Sauté the garlic, ginger, salt and eggs, uncovered, for 1 minute, stirring occasionally.
3. Add the onion and shrimp to the pot and cook for about 1 minute.
4. Toss the peas, sesame oil, rice and soy sauce and stir-fry for 1 minute.
5. When cooking is complete, press START/STOP to end cooking. Sprinkle with the scallions and serve hot.

Chinese Sausage Fried Rice with Peas

PREP TIME: 8 minutes
COOK TIME: 5 minutes

1 tbsp. cooking oil
2 links cured Chinese sausage, sliced into ½-inch pieces
2 cups cold, cooked rice
2 large eggs, beaten
1 cup frozen peas, thawed
4 scallions, cut into ½-inch pieces
2 garlic cloves, crushed and chopped
2 tbsps. soy sauce
1 tbsp. ginger, crushed and chopped
1 tbsp. sesame oil

1. Turn dial to SEAR/SAUTÉ, set temperature to HI, and press START/STOP to begin preheating. Allow the unit to preheat for 5 minutes.
2. When preheating is complete, heat the cooking oil in the pot until it shimmers. Sauté the garlic, ginger and sausage, uncovered, for 1-2 minutes, stirring occasionally.
3. Push the sausage to the sides of the pot, then add the eggs and stir-fry for about 1 minute.
4. Put the rice, peas, soy sauce and sesame oil and cook for 1 minute, stirring frequently.
5. When cooking is complete, press START/STOP to end cooking. Garnish with the scallions and serve warm.

Healthy Quinoa with Brussels Sprouts

PREP TIME: 20 minutes
COOK TIME: 6 hours

3 cups Brussels sprouts
2 cups quinoa, rinsed
1 cup broken walnuts
1 onion, finely chopped
4 cups roasted vegetable broth
2 avocados, peeled and sliced
½ cup pomegranate seeds
3 garlic cloves, minced
1 tsp. dried marjoram leaves
2 tbsps. lemon juice

1. Place the quinoa, onion, garlic, vegetable broth, Brussels sprouts, marjoram, and lemon juice in the pot. Gently stir to combine well, then cover with the lid.
2. Turn dial to SLOW COOK, set temperature to LOW, and set time to 6 hours. Press START/STOP to begin cooking, until the quinoa is soft.
3. When cooking is complete, add the avocado, pomegranate seeds and walnuts and stir to combine. Serve hot.

Herb Barley Risotto with Lemon

SERVES: 1

PREP TIME: 10 minutes
COOK TIME: 7 hours

1 tsp. extra-virgin olive oil
2 cups low-sodium vegetable broth
¾ cup pearl barley
½ cup minced onion
¼ cup roughly chopped fresh parsley, divided
2 tbsps. minced preserved lemon
1 tsp. fresh thyme leaves
⅛ tsp. sea salt
Freshly ground black pepper
½ lemon cut, into wedges, for garnish

1. Lightly grease the inside of the pot with olive oil.
2. Place the preserved lemon, onion, thyme, 2 tbsps. of the parsley, vegetable broth and barley in the pot. Season with the salt and pepper, and stir thoroughly, then cover with the lid.
3. Turn dial to SLOW COOK, set temperature to LOW, and set time to 7 hours. Press START/STOP to begin cooking, until the barley is tender and all the liquid is absorbed.
4. When cooking is complete, garnish with the remaining parsley and a lemon wedge and serve hot.

Mexican Black Bean Quinoa

SERVES: 6

PREP TIME: 10 minutes
COOK TIME: 8 hours

1 (14-ounce, 397 g) can diced tomatoes and peppers, drained
2 cups uncooked quinoa
2 cups cooked black beans, rinsed
2 cups fresh or frozen corn
4 cups (960 ml) vegetable broth
2 jalapeño peppers, seeded and chopped
1 red bell pepper, seeded and chopped
1 green bell pepper, seeded and chopped
¼ cup chopped fresh cilantro
1 tsp. ground cumin

1. Rinse the quinoa in a fine-mesh colander under running water.
2. Add the black beans, quinoa, tomatoes and peppers, broth, jalapeños, corn, bell peppers, and cumin in the pot. Gently stir to combine, then cover with the lid.
3. Turn dial to SLOW COOK, set temperature to LOW, and set time to 8 hours. Press START/STOP to begin cooking.
4. When cooking is complete, add the chopped cilantro just before serving

Indian Fried Rice with Onion

SERVES: 4

PREP TIME: 10 minutes COOK TIME: 3-4 minutes	2 tbsps. cooking oil 2 cups cold, cooked basmati rice 1 medium onion, diced 2 bird's eye chiles, sliced into ¼-inch circles ¼ cup coarsely chopped mint leaves 2 garlic cloves, crushed and chopped 1 tbsp. ginger, crushed and chopped 1 tsp. hot sesame oil 1 tsp. mustard seeds ½ tsp. turmeric ½ tsp. ground coriander ¼ tsp. kosher salt

1. Turn dial to SEAR/SAUTÉ, set temperature to HI, and press START/STOP to begin preheating. Allow the unit to preheat for 5 minutes.
2. When preheating is complete, heat the cooking oil in the pot until it shimmers. Sauté the onion, ginger, mustard seeds and garlic, uncovered, for about 2 minutes, stirring occasionally.
3. Add the bird's eye chiles, sesame oil, coriander, turmeric, salt and rice to the pot and stir-fry for 1 minute.
4. When cooking is complete, press START/STOP to end cooking. Sprinkle with the mint and serve hot.

Kimchi Fried Rice with Mushroom

SERVES: 4

PREP TIME: 12 minutes COOK TIME: 6 minutes	½ pound (227 g) thick-sliced bacon, cut into 1-inch pieces 4 large eggs 2 cups cold, cooked rice 1 cup kimchi, cut into ½-inch pieces ¼ cup kimchi juice 4 ounces (113 g) sliced mushrooms 4 scallions, cut into ½-inch pieces 2 garlic cloves, crushed and chopped 1 tbsp. ginger, crushed and chopped 1 tbsp. soy sauce 1 tsp. sesame oil

1. Turn dial to SEAR/SAUTÉ, set temperature to HI, and press START/STOP to begin preheating. Allow the unit to preheat for 5 minutes.
2. When preheating is complete, add the bacon, ginger and garlic to the pot. Sauté uncovered for 2 minutes, or until the bacon is lightly browned.
3. Drain off all but 2 tbsps. of the bacon fat from the pot and let rest.
4. Add the mushrooms to the pot and stir-fry for about 1 minute.
5. Place the kimchi and cook for 30 seconds.
6. Toss the rice, soy sauce, sesame oil, scallions and kimchi juice in the pot. Stir-fry for about 30 seconds, then transfer to a serving dish.
7. Return 2 tbsps. of the reserved bacon fat to the pot and fry the eggs sunny-side up.
8. When cooking is complete, press START/STOP to end cooking. Top the fried eggs over the rice and serve hot.

Mixed Nut Pilaf with Herbes

SERVES: 4

PREP TIME: 30 minutes
COOK TIME: 20 minutes

2 tbsps. olive oil
1¼ cups basmati rice, rinsed
1 onion, minced
½ cup nuts (pistachios, cashews, slivered almonds)
2 cups chicken broth
2 garlic cloves, minced
1 tbsp. chopped cilantro
1 bay leaf
2 tsps. coriander powder
1 tsp. cumin seed
½ tsp. cardamom
Salt and pepper

1. Soak the rice in a bowl of the fresh cold water for about 30 minutes. Drain the rice well.
2. Turn dial to SEAR/SAUTÉ, set temperature to HI, and press START/STOP to begin preheating. Allow the unit to preheat for 5 minutes.
3. When preheating is complete, heat the olive oil in the pot. Sauté the onion and garlic, uncovered, for 3-5 minutes, stirring occasionally.
4. Add the rice, bay leaf, cumin seeds, coriander and cardamom to the pot and cook for 2 minutes, stirring occasionally.
5. Toss in the broth, salt and pepper and bring to a boil. Cook covered for 8 minutes.
6. When cooking is complete, press START/STOP to end cooking. Let sit covered for 5 minutes
7. Sprinkle with the nuts and toss to coat well. Garnish with the chopped cilantro and serve warm.

Indonesian Tomato Egg Fried Rice

SERVES: 4

PREP TIME: 6 minutes
COOK TIME: 5 minutes

3 tbsps. cooking oil, divided
2 cups cold, cooked rice
½ pound (227 g) ground meat of your choice
4 eggs
1 medium onion, diced
2 tomatoes, sliced
1 cucumber, sliced
4 scallions, cut into ½-inch pieces
2 garlic cloves, crushed and chopped
¼ cup kecap manis
1 tbsp. ginger, crushed and chopped
1 tsp. hot sesame oil

1. Turn dial to SEAR/SAUTÉ, set temperature to HI, and press START/STOP to begin preheating. Allow the unit to preheat for 5 minutes.
2. When preheating is complete, heat 2 tbsps. of the cooking oil in the pot until it shimmers. Sauté the meat, garlic, ginger and onion, uncovered, for about 2 minutes, stirring occasionally.
3. Add the rice, sesame oil, kecap manis and scallions to the pot and cook for 1 minute. Transfer to a serving bowl.
4. Pour the remaining 1 tbsp. of cooking oil to the pot and, once the oil is shimmering, fry the eggs sunny-side up.
5. When cooking is complete, press START/STOP to end cooking. Put a fried egg on top of rice, and sliced cucumbers and tomatoes on the side. Serve warm.

Slow-Cooked Rice with Cheddar

SERVES: 8 TO 10

PREP TIME: 10 to 15 minutes COOK TIME: 3 hours	3 tbsps. butter 2 cups brown rice, uncooked 2 cups shredded cheddar cheese 1 cup slivered almonds, optional ½ cup thinly sliced green onions or shallots 5 cups water 1 tsp. salt ½ tsp. pepper

1. Place the butter, rice, green onion, and salt in the pot and combine well.
2. Bring a pot of water to a boil and pour over the rice mixture into the pot. Then cover with the lid.
3. Turn dial to SLOW COOK, set temperature to HI, and set time to 3 hours. Press START/STOP to begin cooking, until the rice is tender and the liquid is absorbed.
4. With 5 minutes remaining, stir in the pepper and cheese. Cover the lid and continue to cook for 5 minutes.
5. When cooking is complete, garnish with the slivered almonds, if desired.

Wild Rice with Chili and Vegetable

SERVES: 8

PREP TIME: 20 minutes COOK TIME: 6 hours	2 (15-ounce (425g)) BPA-free cans no-salt-added black beans, drained and rinsed 1½ cups wild rice, rinsed and drained 2 cups sliced cremini mushrooms 2 red bell peppers, stemmed, seeded, and chopped 2 onions, chopped 5 cups roasted vegetable broth 3 cups low-sodium tomato juice 3 garlic cloves, minced 1 tbsp. chili powder ½ tsp. ground cumin

1. Add all the ingredients in the pot. Gently stir to combine, then cover with the lid.
2. Turn dial to SLOW COOK, set temperature to LOW, and set time to 6 hours. Press START/STOP to begin cooking, until the wild rice is soft.
3. When cooking is complete, remove the lid and serve immediately.

CHAPTER 4
FISH AND SEAFOOD

Curried Shrimp with Basmati

SERVES: 5

PREP TIME: 25 minutes
COOK TIME: 20 minutes

2 tbsps. olive oil
1 pound (454 g) large shrimp, peeled and deveined
2 stalks celery, strings removed, diced
1 small onion, diced
2 oranges, zest and juice
1 cup tomato juice
½ cup heavy cream
Cooked basmati rice
1 tbsp. hot curry powder
1 tsp. dried oregano
Coarse salt
Ground black pepper

1. Turn dial to SEAR/SAUTÉ, set temperature to HI, and press START/STOP to begin preheating. Allow the unit to preheat for 5 minutes.
2. Meanwhile, mix together the shrimp, half of the orange zest, 1½ tsps. of the curry powder, ¼ tsp. of the salt and ¼ tsp. of the pepper in a large bowl.
3. When preheating is complete, heat 1 tbsp. of the oil in the pot. Sear the shrimp, uncovered, for 1-2 minutes per side. Transfer the shrimp to a plate.
4. Heat the remaining oil in the pot and add the celery, onion, dried oregano and remaining 1½ tsps. of the curry powder. Cook for about 4 minutes.
5. Toss in the orange and tomato juices and cook for 8 minutes.
6. Return the cooked shrimp to the pot and cook for about 2 minutes.
7. Stir in the remaining orange zest, heavy cream, salt and pepper.
8. When cooking is complete, press START/STOP to end cooking. Serve over cooked basmati rice.

Garlic King Crab with Hoisin Sauce

SERVES: 6

PREP TIME: 12 minutes
COOK TIME: 6 minutes

3 tbsps. cooking oil
2 pounds (907 g) king crab legs, cut into 2-inch sections and left in the shell
1 cup fish or lobster broth
¼ cup hoisin sauce
4 scallions, cut into ½-inch pieces
3 garlic cloves, crushed and chopped
2 tbsps. ginger, crushed and chopped
2 tbsps. rice wine
2 tbsps. cornstarch

1. Turn dial to SEAR/SAUTÉ, set temperature to HI, and press START/STOP to begin preheating. Allow the unit to preheat for 5 minutes.
2. Meanwhile, whisk together the broth, rice wine and cornstarch in a small bowl and set aside.
3. When preheating is complete, heat the cooking oil in the pot until it shimmers. Sauté the garlic and ginger, uncovered, for about 1 minute, stirring occasionally.
4. Add the crab legs to the pot and stir-fry for about 1 minute.
5. Pour in the broth mixture and cook for about 1 minute.
6. Toss the hoisin sauce and stir-fry until a glaze forms.
7. Squeeze the scallions to bruise them, then scatter them into the pot to garnish the crab.
8. When cooking is complete, press START/STOP to end cooking. Serve hot.

Mussels with Tomato Sauce

PREP TIME: 20 minutes
COOK TIME: 20 minutes

1 tbsp. olive oil
1 tbsp. clarified butter
1 pound (454 g) mussels, cleaned and debearded
1 cup chopped green onions
3 cups canned tomato sauce
2 tbsps. minced shallots
2 tbsps. minced garlic
1 tbsp. capers
1 tbsp. Italian seasoning
½ tsp. red pepper flakes

1. Turn dial to SEAR/SAUTÉ, set temperature to HI, and press START/STOP to begin preheating. Allow the unit to preheat for 5 minutes.
2. When preheating is complete, heat the oil and butter in the pot. Sauté the shallots, garlic and capers, uncovered, for about 3-4 minutes, stirring occasionally.
3. Toss in the tomato sauce, Italian herbs and red pepper flakes. Cover and cook for 6-8 minutes.
4. Stir in the mussels and cook covered for about 8 minutes.
5. Scoop out and discard any unopened mussels from the pot.
6. When cooking is complete, press START/STOP to end cooking. Garnish the green onions and serve warm.

Garlic & Herbs Cod

PREP TIME: 10 minutes
COOK TIME: 1½ hours

1 tbsp. olive oil
2 medium cod fillets
2 garlic cloves, minced
2 tbsps. unsalted butter
Juice of 1 lemon

1 tbsp. fresh rosemary, chopped
1 tbsp. fresh thyme, chopped
Salt and pepper to taste
white rice, for serving

1. Before getting started, add 12 cups of room-temperature water to the pot.
2. Cover with the lid and turn dial to SOUS VIDE, set temperature to 130°F and set time to 1½ hours. Press START/STOP to begin preheating.
3. Rub the cod fillets with salt and pepper to taste, and put them into the Sous Vide bag, adding the thyme, rosemary, butter, minced garlic and lemon juice.
4. When preheating is complete and "ADD FOOD" will show on the display.
5. Open the lid. Place the bag in water and seal it using the water displacement method. Close the lid.
6. When cooking is complete, remove the bag with fish from the pot.
7. Pour off any remaining water and pat the pot dry with a paper towel. Turn dial to SEAR/SAUTÉ, set temperature to HI, and press START/STOP to begin preheating. Allow the unit to preheat for 5 minutes.
8. When preheating is complete, heat 1 tbsp. olive oil in the pot. Place the fish in the pot and sear both sides.
9. Serve over white rice.

Herbed Lemon Flounder

PREP TIME: 5 minutes
COOK TIME: 6 hours

2 lbs. (907 g) flounder fillets, fresh or frozen
4 tbsps. chopped fresh parsley
¾ cup chicken broth
2 tbsps. lemon juice
2 tbsps. dried chives
2 tbsps. dried minced onion
½–1 tsp. leaf marjoram
½ tsp. salt

1. Pat the fish as dry as possible with the paper towel. Cut fish into portions to fit the pot.
2. Season the fish with the salt to taste.
3. In a small bowl, combine the lemon juice and broth. Stir in the onion, chives, parsley and leaf marjoram.
4. Add the fish in the pot and pour the mixture over, then cover with the lid.
5. Turn dial to SLOW COOK, set temperature to LOW, and set time to 6 hours. Press START/STOP to begin cooking.
6. When cooking is complete, remove the lid and serve immediately.

Shrimp Slow Cooked with Grits

PREP TIME: 20 minutes
COOK TIME: 6 hours

2 pounds (907g) raw shrimp, peeled and deveined
2½ cups stone-ground grits
1½ cups shredded Cheddar cheese
4 large tomatoes, seeded and chopped
2 green bell peppers, stemmed, seeded, and chopped
2 onions, chopped
8 cups chicken stock or roasted vegetable broth
5 garlic cloves, minced
1 bay leaf
1 tsp. Old Bay Seasoning

1. Place the grits, onions, garlic, tomatoes, sweet peppers, chicken broth, bay leaves, and seasonings in the pot. Gently stir to combine, then cover with the lid.
2. Turn dial to SLOW COOK, set temperature to LOW, and set time to 6 hours. Press START/STOP to begin cooking.
3. With 30 minutes remaining, add the shrimp and continue to cook for 30 minutes, until the shrimp turns pink.
4. When cooking is complete, stir in the cheese and serve immediately.

Teriyaki Salmon with Sugar Snap

SERVES: 4

PREP TIME: 9 minutes
COOK TIME: 6 minutes

2 tbsps. cooking oil
1 pound (454 g) thick, center-cut salmon fillet, cut into 1-inch pieces
2 cups sugar snap or snow pea pods
1 medium onion, diced
4 ounces (113 g) shiitake mushrooms, cut into slices
2 scallions, cut into 1-inch pieces
2 garlic cloves, crushed and chopped
2 tbsps. honey
2 tbsps. mirin
2 tbsps. tamari
2 tbsps. rice vinegar
1 tbsp. white miso
1 tbsp. ginger, crushed and chopped
1 tbsp. sesame seeds

1. In a large bowl, whisk together the tamari, honey, mirin, rice vinegar and miso. Place the salmon, making sure to coat evenly with the marinade, and set aside.
2. Turn dial to SEAR/SAUTÉ, set temperature to HI, and press START/STOP to begin preheating. Allow the unit to preheat for 5 minutes.
3. When preheating is complete, heat the cooking oil in the pot until it shimmers. Sauté the ginger, garlic and onion, uncovered, for 1-2 minutes, stirring occasionally.
4. Add the mushrooms and pea pods to the pot and stir-fry for 1 minute.
5. Then add the marinated salmon, reserving the marinade, and cook for about 1 minute.
6. Toss in the marinade and scallions and stir to coat for 30 seconds.
7. When cooking is complete, press START/STOP to end cooking. Sprinkle the sesame seeds on top. Serve hot.

Sweet Vietnamese Scallops and Cucumbers

SERVES: 4

PREP TIME: 10 minutes
COOK TIME: 3 minutes

2 tbsps. cooking oil
1 pound (454 g) large sea scallops, cut in half widthwise
1 European cucumber, raked and cut into ¼-inch disks
¼ cup brown sugar
¼ cup fish sauce
¼ cup rice wine
¼ cup rice vinegar
Juice of 1 lime
1 tsp. hot sesame oil
4 scallions, cut into 1-inch pieces
2 garlic cloves, crushed and chopped

1. Combine the fish sauce, rice wine, brown sugar, and lime juice in a large bowl. Add the scallops to marinate and set aside.
2. Turn dial to SEAR/SAUTÉ, set temperature to HI, and press START/STOP to begin preheating. Allow the unit to preheat for 5 minutes.
3. When preheating is complete, heat the cooking oil in the pot until it shimmers. Sauté the scallions and garlic, uncovered, for about 30 seconds, stirring occasionally.
4. Place the marinated scallops to the pot, reserving the marinade, and stir-fry for about about 1 minute.
5. Then pour the cucumber and marinade to the pot and cook for about 1 minute.
6. When cooking is complete, press START/STOP to end cooking. Toss the cucumbers and scallops with the sesame oil and rice vinegar. Serve warm.

Salmon and Vegetables with Oyster Sauce

SERVES: 4

PREP TIME: 9 minutes COOK TIME: 6 minutes	2 tbsps. cooking oil 1 pound (454 g) thick, center-cut salmon fillet, cut into 1-inch pieces 1 red bell pepper, cut into 1-inch pieces 1 red onion, cut into 1-inch pieces 2 baby bok choy, leaves separated ½ cup oyster sauce 4 scallions, cut into ½-inch pieces 2 garlic cloves, crushed and chopped 2 tbsps. rice wine 1 tbsp. crushed and chopped ginger

1. Whisk together the oyster sauce and rice wine in a large bowl. Add the salmon to marinate and set aside.
2. Turn dial to SEAR/SAUTÉ, set temperature to HI, and press START/STOP to begin preheating. Allow the unit to preheat for 5 minutes.
3. When preheating is complete, heat the cooking oil in the pot until it shimmers. Sauté the ginger, garlic and onion, uncovered, for 1-2 minutes, stirring occasionally.
4. Place the salmon to the pot, reserving the marinade, and slowly stir-fry for about 1 minute.
5. Then put the bell pepper and bok choy and cook for about 1 minute.
6. Pour the reserved marinade and scallions to the pot and cook for 1 minute.
7. When cooking is complete, press START/STOP to end cooking. Serve warm.

Shrimps Cajun

SERVES: 4

PREP TIME: 10 minutes COOK TIME: 30 minutes	1 tbsp. olive oil 16 shrimps, peeled and deveined 2 garlic cloves, minced 4 tbsps. freshly chopped parsley 1 shallot, minced 1 tbsp. unsalted butter, melted 1 tbsp. Cajun seasoning 1 tbsp. lemon juice Freshly ground black pepper to taste

1. Before getting started, add 12 cups of room-temperature water to the pot.
2. Cover with the lid and turn dial to SOUS VIDE, set temperature to 130°F and set time to 30 minutes. Press START/STOP to begin preheating.
3. Add all the ingredients except parsley and olive oil into a Sous Vide bag.
4. When preheating is complete and "ADD FOOD" will show on the display.
5. Open the lid. Place the bag in water and seal it using the water displacement method. Close the lid.
6. When cooking is complete, remove the bag with shrimps from the pot.
7. Pour off any remaining water and pat the pot dry with a paper towel. Turn dial to SEAR/SAUTÉ, set temperature to HI, and press START/STOP to begin preheating. Allow the unit to preheat for 5 minutes.
8. When preheating is complete, heat the olive oil in the pot. Place the shrimps in the pot and cook for about 30 seconds, until crispy.
9. Serve garnished with the chopped parsley.

Aromatic Shrimps

SERVES: 2

PREP TIME: 10 minutes COOK TIME: 30 minutes	1 tsp. olive oil 1 pound large shrimps, peeled and deveined 2 tbsps. lemon juice 1 tbsp. unsalted vegan butter Any aromatics of your choice Salt to taste

1. Before getting started, add 12 cups of room-temperature water to the pot.
2. Cover with the lid and turn dial to SOUS VIDE, set temperature to 130°F and set time to 30 minutes. Press START/STOP to begin preheating.
3. Season the shrimps with salt and put into the Sous Vide bag. Add 1 tsp. olive oil and aromatics.
4. When preheating is complete and "ADD FOOD" will show on the display.
5. Open the lid. Place the bag in water and seal it using the water displacement method. Close the lid.
6. When cooking is complete, remove the bag with shrimps from the pot.
7. Pour off any remaining water and pat the pot dry with a paper towel. Turn dial to SEAR/SAUTÉ, set temperature to HI, and press START/STOP to begin preheating. Allow the unit to preheat for 5 minutes.
8. When preheating is complete, melt the butter in the pot. Place the shrimps in the pot and cook for about 30 seconds, until the shrimps are heated.
9. Serve with any sauce of your choice or sprinkled with lemon juice.

Healthy Salmon with Root Vegetables

SERVES: 6

PREP TIME: 20 minutes
COOK TIME: 4½ hours
	6 (5-ounce (142g)) salmon fillets
	4 large carrots, sliced
	4 Yukon Gold potatoes, cubed
	2 sweet potatoes, peeled and
	   cubed
	2 onions, chopped
		3 garlic cloves, minced
		⅓ cup grated Parmesan cheese
		⅓ cup roasted vegetable broth
		   or fish stock
		1 tsp. dried thyme leaves
		½ tsp. salt

1. Place the carrots, sweet potatoes, Yukon golden potatoes, onions, garlic, vegetable broth, thyme, and salt in the pot. Gently stir to combine, then cover with the lid.
2. Turn dial to SLOW COOK, set temperature to LOW, and set time to 4½ hours. Press START/STOP to begin cooking.
3. With 20 minutes remaining, add the salmon fillets and sprinkle with some cheese, until the salmon fillets are cooked through.
4. When cooking is complete, remove the lid and serve immediately.

Fish Feast with Mixed Veggies

SERVES: 8

PREP TIME: 10 minutes
COOK TIME: 5 hours
	1 tbsp. olive oil
	3 lbs. (1.4 kg) red snapper fillets
	14-oz. (397 g) can low-sodium diced
	   tomatoes
	1 large onion, sliced
	2 unpeeled zucchini, sliced
	1 green bell pepper, cut in 1-inch pieces
		¼ cup dry white wine or white
		   grape juice
		1 tbsp. garlic, minced
		½ tsp. dried oregano
		½ tsp. dried basil
		¼ tsp. salt
		¼ tsp. black pepper

1. Lightly grease the inside of the pot with olive oil.
2. Rinse the snapper and use paper towel to pat dry. Place the fish in the pot.
3. In a large bowl, combine the remaining ingredients together and pour over the fish in the pot. Then cover with the lid.
4. Turn dial to SLOW COOK, set temperature to LOW, and set time to 5 hours. Press START/STOP to begin cooking.
5. When cooking is complete, remove the lid and serve immediately.

CHAPTER 5
BEEF, LAMB AND PORK

Pork and Bok Choy with Oyster Sauce

PREP TIME: 6 minutes
COOK TIME: 5 minutes

2 tbsps. cooking oil
1 pound (454 g) ground pork
2 cups chopped bok choy
4 scallions, cut into 1-inch pieces
2 garlic cloves, crushed and chopped
¼ cup oyster sauce
1 tbsp. Chinese five-spice powder
1 tbsp. ginger, crushed and chopped
1 tsp. hot sesame oil

1. Turn dial to SEAR/SAUTÉ, set temperature to HI, and press START/STOP to begin preheating. Allow the unit to preheat for 5 minutes.
2. When preheating is complete, heat the cooking oil in the pot until it shimmers. Sauté the garlic, ginger, pork and five-spice powder, uncovered, for about 1-2 minutes, stirring occasionally.
3. Add the sesame oil and bok choy to the pot and stir-fry for about 1 minute.
4. Pour the oyster sauce, toss to coat well and sauté for about 30 seconds.
5. When cooking is complete, press START/STOP to end cooking. Sprinkle with the scallions and serve warm.

Sweet and Sour Beef Stir Fry

PREP TIME: 25 minutes
COOK TIME: 15 minutes

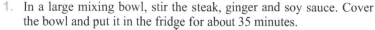

4 cups cooked rice
1 pound (454 g) round steak, thinly sliced
12 mushrooms, sliced
1 red bell pepper, chopped
1 onion, chopped
¼ cup sweet and sour sauce
1 (1 inch) piece fresh ginger root, peeled and thinly sliced
1 tbsp. soy sauce
1 tsp. butter

1. In a large mixing bowl, stir the steak, ginger and soy sauce. Cover the bowl and put it in the fridge for about 35 minutes.
2. Turn dial to SEAR/SAUTÉ, set temperature to HI, and press START/STOP to begin preheating. Allow the unit to preheat for 5 minutes.
3. When preheating is complete, add the steak mixture in the pot. Sauté for 3-5 minutes, stirring occasionally. Drain the beef and set aside.
4. Heat the butter in the pot until it melts. Place the onion, bell pepper, mushrooms and sweet and sour sauce and cook for about 4 minutes.
5. Return the beef into the pot and cook for about 3 minutes.
6. When cooking is complete, press START/STOP to end cooking. Serve hot with cooked rice.

New York Strip Steak

PREP TIME: 5 minutes
COOK TIME: 1 hour

1 tbsp. olive oil
1 New York Strip Steak
2 tbsps. dried rosemary and thyme
Salt and pepper as needed
Steak seasoning as you prefer

1. Before getting started, add 12 cups of room-temperature water to the pot.
2. Cover with the lid and turn dial to SOUS VIDE, set temperature to 145°F and set time to 1 hour. Press START/STOP to begin preheating.
3. Season the steak with pepper and salt to taste and place the herbs on top. Add it in a zip bag.
4. When preheating is complete and "ADD FOOD" will show on the display.
5. Open the lid. Place the bag in water and seal it using the water displacement method. Close the lid.
6. When cooking is complete, remove the bag with steak from the pot. Pat dry the steak.
7. Pour off any remaining water and pat the pot dry with a paper towel. Turn dial to SEAR/SAUTÉ, set temperature to HI, and press START/STOP to begin preheating. Allow the unit to preheat for 5 minutes.
8. When preheating is complete, heat the olive oil in the pot. Place the steak in the pot and sear both sides until the steak is browned.
9. Slice and serve!

Teriyaki Skewered Lamb

PREP TIME: 10 minutes
COOK TIME: 3 hours

2 tbsps. sesame oil
2 lamb loin steaks, cut into 2-inch cubes
1 tbsp. mirin
1 tbsp. soy sauce

1. Before getting started, add 12 cups of room-temperature water to the pot.
2. Cover with the lid and turn dial to SOUS VIDE, set temperature to 145°F and set time to 3 hours. Press START/STOP to begin preheating.
3. In a Sous Vide bag, combine the lamb, soy sauce and mirin.
4. When preheating is complete and "ADD FOOD" will show on the display.
5. Open the lid. Place the bag in water and seal it using the water displacement method. Close the lid.
6. When cooking is complete, remove the bag with lamb from the pot. Pat the lamb dry with kitchen towel. Thread onto skewers and discard the cooking liquid.
7. Pour off any remaining water and pat the pot dry with a paper towel. Turn dial to SEAR/SAUTÉ, set temperature to HI, and press START/STOP to begin preheating. Allow the unit to preheat for 5 minutes.
8. When preheating is complete, heat the oil in the pot. Place the lamb in the pot and sear both sides.
9. Serve hot.

Braised Lamb Shanks with Veggies

SERVES: 4 TO 6

PREP TIME: 10 minutes
COOK TIME: 4 hours 15 minutes

1 tbsp. olive oil
3 lamb shanks, cracked
2 small carrots, cut in thin strips
1 medium onion, thinly sliced
1 rib celery, chopped
1–2 cloves garlic, split
8-oz. (227 g) can tomato sauce

2 cups beef broth
½ cup dry white wine
2 bay leaves, crumbled
1 tsp. dried thyme
1 tsp. dried oregano
1½ tsps. salt
¼ tsp. pepper

1. Turn dial to SEAR/SAUTÉ, set temperature to HI, and press START/STOP to begin preheating. Allow the unit to preheat for 5 minutes.
2. While unit is preheating, rub the lamb with garlic and season with salt and pepper.
3. When preheating is complete, add the oil in the pot. Place the lamb shanks in the pot and brown for about 10 minutes.
4. After 10 minutes, use tongs to remove the lamb shanks from the pot and set aside.
5. Add the carrots, onions, and celery to the pot. Cook for 5 minutes, stirring frequently.
6. Add the tomato sauce, beef broth, dry white wine, thyme, oregano and bay leaves to the pot. Stir to combine.
7. Place the lamb shanks back into the pot. Nestle the lamb into the vegetables, then cover with the lid.
8. Turn dial to BRAISE, set time to 4 hours, and press START/STOP to resume cooking.
9. When cooking is complete, remove the lid and let cool for 5 minutes before serving.

Balsamic Braised Beef Short Ribs

SERVES: 8

PREP TIME: 10 minutes
COOK TIME: 4 hours 20 minutes

1 tbsp. extra-virgin olive oil
2 pounds (907 g) beef short ribs
1 sweet onion, sliced
2 cups beef broth
2 tbsps. granulated erythritol
2 tbsps. balsamic vinegar
2 tsps. dried thyme
1 tsp. hot sauce

1. Turn dial to SEAR/SAUTÉ, set temperature to HI, and press START/STOP to begin preheating. Allow the unit to preheat for 5 minutes.
2. While unit is preheating, season the ribs with salt and pepper on both sides.
3. When preheating is complete, heat the oil in the pot. Place the ribs in the pot and brown for about 15 minutes.
4. After 15 minutes, use tongs to remove the ribs from the pot and set aside.
5. Add the onion to the pot and cook for 5 minutes, stirring frequently.
6. Add the broth, balsamic vinegar, erythritol, thyme, and hot sauce to the pot. Stir to combine.
7. Place the ribs into the pot. Nestle the ribs into the onion and sauce mixture, then cover with the lid.
8. Turn dial to BRAISE, set time to 4 hours, and press START/STOP to resume cooking.
9. When cooking is complete, remove the lid and let cool for 5 minutes before serving.

Fried Beef and Butternut Squash

PREP TIME: 20 minutes COOK TIME: 20 minutes	1 (8-ounce / 227-g) package dry Chinese noodles 1 pound (454 g) flank beef steak, cut diagonally into 2 inch strips ½ small butternut squash, peeled, seeded, and thinly sliced 3 cups cabbage, thinly sliced 1 cup sliced fresh mushrooms 1 large red onion, cut into 2 inch strips 1 tangerine, sectioned and seeded ¼ cup dry sherry ¼ cup hoisin sauce 2 tbsps. canola oil 1 tsp. tangerine zest ¼ tsp. ground ginger

1. According to the directions on the package, cook the noodles.
2. Turn dial to SEAR/SAUTÉ, set temperature to HI, and press START/STOP to begin preheating. Allow the unit to preheat for 5 minutes.
3. Meanwhile, mix the hoisin sauce, sherry, tangerine zest and ground ginger in a small bowl.
4. When preheating is complete, heat 1 tbsp. canola oil in the pot. Sauté the beef, uncovered, for 5-6 minutes, stirring occasionally. Set aside.
5. Heat the rest of the oil in the pot. Cook the mushrooms, butternut squash and onion for about 6 minutes.
6. Stir in the cabbage and sauté for about 3 minutes, stirring occasionally.
7. Place the beef, tangerine sections and hoisin mixture and cook for about 4 minutes.
8. When cooking is complete, press START/STOP to end cooking. Serve hot.

Sweet Lamb and Cabbage

PREP TIME: 7 minutes COOK TIME: 6 minutes	2 tbsps. cooking oil 1 pound (454 g) boneless leg of lamb or shoulder, cut into ¼-inch strips 1 cup Napa cabbage, shredded 1 medium onion, diced 2 garlic cloves, crushed and chopped ¼ cup rice vinegar 2 tbsps. soy sauce 2 tbsps. brown sugar 2 tbsps. cornstarch 1 tbsp. ginger, crushed and chopped 1 tsp. red pepper flakes

1. Turn dial to SEAR/SAUTÉ, set temperature to HI, and press START/STOP to begin preheating. Allow the unit to preheat for 5 minutes.
2. In a small bowl, whisk together the soy sauce, rice vinegar, brown sugar and cornstarch. Keep aside.
3. When preheating is complete, heat the cooking oil in the pot until it shimmers. Sauté the garlic, ginger, lamb, onion and red pepper flakes, uncovered, for about 3 minutes, stirring occasionally.
4. Add the soy sauce mixture and cabbage to the pot and stir until a glaze is formed.
5. When cooking is complete, press START/STOP to end cooking. Serve warm.

Hoisin Glazed Pork Tenderloin

SERVES: 3

PREP TIME: 20 minutes
COOK TIME: 3 hours 5 minutes

1 tbsp. olive oil
1-piece pork tenderloin, trimmed
3 tbsps. hoisin sauce
1 tsp. kosher salt
½ tsp. freshly ground black pepper

1. Before getting started, add 12 cups of room-temperature water to the pot.
2. Cover with the lid and turn dial to SOUS VIDE, set temperature to 145°F and set time to 3 hours. Press START/STOP to begin preheating.
3. Season the tenderloin with pepper and salt and transfer to a resealable zip bag.
4. When preheating is complete and "ADD FOOD" will show on the display.
5. Open the lid. Place the bag in water and seal it using the water displacement method. Close the lid.
6. When cooking is complete, remove the bag with tenderloin from the pot. Brush the pork with hoisin sauce.
7. Pour off any remaining water and pat the pot dry with a paper towel. Turn dial to SEAR/SAUTÉ, set temperature to HI, and press START/STOP to begin preheating. Allow the unit to preheat for 5 minutes.
8. When preheating is complete, heat the olive oil in the pot. Place the tenderloin in the pot and sear for 5 minutes, until all sides are caramelized.
9. Let rest and slice the tenderloin into medallions. Serve!

Chili Pork Chops

SERVES: 2

PREP TIME: 5 minutes
COOK TIME: 1 hour

1 tbsp. vegetable oil
2 pork rib chops
1 small onion, chopped
2 garlic cloves
2 tbsps. Worcestershire sauce
1 tbsp. unsalted butter
½ tsp. chili powder
Salt and pepper to taste

1. Before getting started, add 12 cups of room-temperature water to the pot.
2. Cover with the lid and turn dial to SOUS VIDE, set temperature to 145°F and set time to 1 hour. Press START/STOP to begin preheating.
3. In a small bowl, mix the salt, pepper and chili powder.
4. Rub the pork chops with the seasonings and put them into the Sous Vide bag.
5. Add the chopped onion, garlic cloves, Worcestershire sauce and olive oil to the bag.
6. When preheating is complete and "ADD FOOD" will show on the display.
7. Open the lid. Place the bag in water and seal it using the water displacement method. Close the lid.
8. When cooking is complete, remove the bag with chops from the pot. Pat the chops dry with the paper towels.
9. Pour off any remaining water and pat the pot dry with a paper towel. Turn dial to SEAR/SAUTÉ, set temperature to HI, and press START/STOP to begin preheating. Allow the unit to preheat for 5 minutes.
10. When preheating is complete, melt 1 tbsp. butter in the pot. Place the chops in the pot and sear on both sides for about 40 seconds, until light brown.
11. Serve hot.

Pork and Sauerkraut Meal

PREP TIME: 5 minutes
COOK TIME: 4 hours

2 lbs. (907 g) thinly sliced lean pork chops, trimmed of fat
2 lbs. (907 g) sauerkraut, rinsed
1 cup water
2 cups low-sodium barbecue sauce

1. Mix the water and barbecue sauce in a bowl, then pour into the pot.
2. Place the sauerkraut and pork chops into the pot. Gently stir to combine, then cover with the lid.
3. Turn dial to SLOW COOK, set temperature to LOW, and set time to 4 hours. Press START/STOP to begin cooking.
4. When cooking is complete, remove the lid and serve immediately.

Italian Braised Veal Shanks

PREP TIME: 10 minutes
COOK TIME: 3 hours 15 minutes

1 tbsp. olive oil
1 veal shank, about 1 pound (454 g)
½ cup diced celery
½ cup diced carrot
½ cup diced onion
1 cup low-sodium chicken or beef broth
½ cup dry red wine
½ tsp. orange zest
1 tsp. fresh thyme
1 tsp. minced garlic
1 tsp. fresh rosemary
½ tbsp. tomato paste
⅛ tsp. sea salt
Freshly ground black pepper

1. In a small bowl, add the thyme, garlic, rosemary, tomato paste, salt and a few grinds of the black pepper and combine together. Coat the veal shank with this mixture.
2. Turn dial to SEAR/SAUTÉ, set temperature to HI, and press START/STOP to begin preheating. Allow the unit to preheat for 5 minutes.
3. When preheating is complete, add the oil in the pot. Place the veal shank in the pot and brown for 8-10 minutes.
4. Once browned, use tongs to remove the veal shank from the pot and set aside.
5. Add the carrot, onion, celery to the pot. Cook for 5 minutes, stirring frequently.
6. Add the wine, orange zest, and broth to the pot. Stir to combine.
7. Place the veal shank back into the pot. Nestle the veal shank into the vegetable and wine mixture, then cover with the lid.
8. Turn dial to BRAISE, set time to 3 hours, and press START/STOP to resume cooking.
9. When cooking is complete, remove the lid and let cool for 5 minutes before serving.

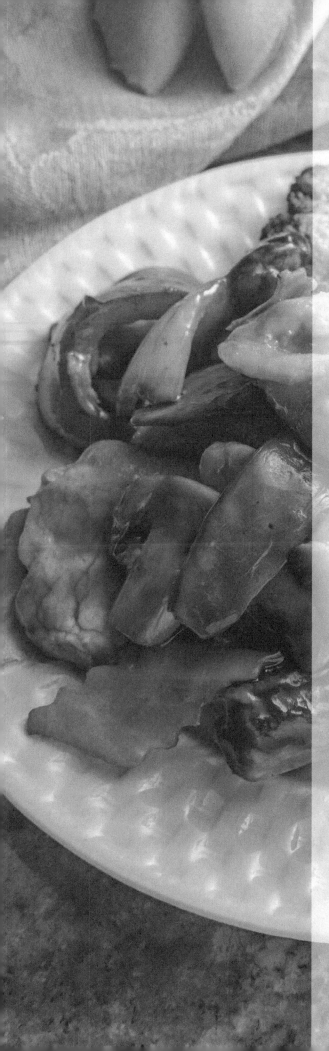

CHAPTER 6
POULTRY

Chicken and Vegetables with Hoisin Sauce

PREP TIME: 8 minutes
COOK TIME: 5 minutes

2 tbsps. cooking oil
1 pound (454 g) ground chicken
2 cups sugar snap or snow pea pods
1 medium onion, cut into 1-inch pieces
1 medium carrot, roll-cut into ½-inch pieces
¼ cup hoisin sauce
2 garlic cloves, crushed and chopped
1 tbsp. ginger, crushed and chopped

1. Turn dial to SEAR/SAUTÉ, set temperature to HI, and press START/STOP to begin preheating. Allow the unit to preheat for 5 minutes.
2. When preheating is complete, heat the cooking oil in the pot until it shimmers. Sauté the garlic, ginger, carrot and chicken, uncovered, for 1-2 minutes, stirring occasionally.
3. Add the onion and pea pods to the pot and cook for about 1-2 minutes.
4. Toss the hoisin sauce and stir-fry for about 30 seconds.
5. When cooking is complete, press START/STOP to end cooking. Serve hot.

Curry Chicken and Potato

PREP TIME: 20 minutes
COOK TIME: 45 minutes

¼ cup canola oil
1 (3-pound / 1.4-kg) chicken, cut into pieces
5 russet potatoes, peeled and cut into 1-inch pieces
2 onions, chopped
8 cloves garlic, chopped
¼ cup mild curry powder
2 tbsps. hot curry powder
1 tsp. ground black pepper
Salt to taste

1. Turn dial to SEAR/SAUTÉ, set temperature to HI, and press START/STOP to begin preheating. Allow the unit to preheat for 5 minutes.
2. When preheating is complete, add the chicken and enough water to cover and bring to a boil in the pot. Cook for 15-18 minutes. Transfer the chicken to a bowl and set aside.
3. Heat the canola oil in the pot and cook the garlic and onion for 3-4 minutes.
4. Stir in both curry powders, salt and black pepper and cook for 4 minutes.
5. Return the chicken back to the pot. Toss the potatoes and simmer for 15-20 minutes.
6. When cooking is complete, press START/STOP to end cooking. Serve warm.

Ginger Duck Breast

PREP TIME: 20 minutes
COOK TIME: 1 hour 30 minutes

1½ tsps. sesame oil
2 boneless duck breasts
1-inch fresh ginger, peeled, sliced thinly
2 garlic cloves, thinly sliced
Kosher salt and pepper

1. Before getting started, add 12 cups of room-temperature water to the pot.
2. Cover with the lid and turn dial to SOUS VIDE, set temperature to 165°F and set time to 1 hour 30 minutes. Press START/STOP to begin preheating.
3. Season the duck breasts with salt and pepper to taste.
4. In a Sous Vide bag, combine the duck breasts with ginger, sesame oil and garlic. Shake to coat the duck breasts evenly.
5. When preheating is complete and "ADD FOOD" will show on the display.
6. Open the lid. Place the bag in water and seal it using the water displacement method. Close the lid.
7. When cooking is complete, remove the duck and discard the garlic, ginger and cooking liquid.
8. Pour off any remaining water and pat the pot dry with a paper towel. Turn dial to SEAR/SAUTÉ, set temperature to HI, and press START/STOP to begin preheating. Allow the unit to preheat for 5 minutes.
9. When preheating is complete, add the duck breasts, skin side down, in the pot. Fry for about 30 seconds on both sides, until light brown.
10. Place the duck breasts on a cutting board to rest for 5 minutes.
11. Slice the duck breasts and serve with your desired side dishes.

Slow Cooked Barbecued Chicken

PREP TIME: 15 minutes
COOK TIME: 8 hours

4 tbsps. butter
6 cups diced cooked chicken
2 cups chopped celery
1 cup chopped green peppers
1 cup chopped onions
2 cups ketchup
2 cups water
4 tbsps. vinegar
2 tbsps. brown sugar
2 tsps. dry mustard
1 tsp. salt
1 tsp. pepper

1. Place the all the ingredients in the pot. Gently stir to combine, then cover with the lid.
2. Turn dial to SLOW COOK, set temperature to LOW, and set time to 8 hours. Press START/STOP to begin cooking.
3. When cooking is complete, stir the chicken until it shreds. Pile into the steak rolls and serve immediately.

Tasty Turkey and Beans

SERVES: 8

PREP TIME: 15 minutes
COOK TIME: 2 hours

1 tbsp. olive oil
1 lb. (454 g) ground turkey
16-oz. (454 g) can kidney beans, drained
16-oz. (454 g) can baked beans, undrained
2 cups onions, chopped
1 cup ketchup
¾ cup brown sugar
2 tbsps. dry mustard
2 tsps. cider vinegar
¼ tsp. sal

1. Turn dial to SEAR/SAUTÉ, set temperature to HI, and press START/STOP to begin preheating. Allow the unit to preheat for 5 minutes.
2. When preheating is complete, heat the olive oil in the pot. Brown the ground turkey, uncovered, for 3-4 minutes, stirring occasionally.
3. Once browned, add the remaining ingredients to the pot. Stir to combine, then cover with the lid.
4. Turn dial to SLOW COOK, set temperature to HI, and set time to 2 hours.
5. When cooking is complete, stir to combine well and serve immediately.

Ginger Peach Chicken

SERVES: 10

PREP TIME: 15 minutes
COOK TIME: 6 hours

Cooking spray
10 boneless skinless chicken thighs (about 2½ pounds, 1.1 kg)
1 cup sliced peeled fresh or frozen peaches
1 cup golden raisins
1 cup peach preserves
⅓ cup chili sauce
2 tbsps. minced crystallized ginger
1 tbsp. reduced-sodium soy sauce
1 tbsp. minced garlic
Hot cooked rice, optional

1. Lightly spray the inside of the pot with cooking spray.
2. Place the chicken, raisins and peaches in the pot.
3. Add the chili sauce, peach preserves, soy sauce, garlic and ginger in a small bowl and combine together. Spoon the mixture over the top of chicken, then cover with the lid.
4. Turn dial to SLOW COOK, set temperature to LOW, and set time to 6 hours. Press START/STOP to begin cooking, until chicken is tender.
5. When cooking is complete, remove the lid. Serve with rice if desired.

Cilantro Chicken Cutlets with Salsa

SERVES: 4

PREP TIME: 5 minutes
COOK TIME: 12 minutes

1 tbsp. ghee
4 boneless skinless chicken breast halves
¼ cup chopped fresh cilantro
½ cup prepared salsa
2 tbsps. fresh lime juice
1 tbsp. Dijon mustard

1. Turn dial to SEAR/SAUTÉ, set temperature to HI, and press START/STOP to begin preheating. Allow the unit to preheat for 5 minutes.
2. While unit is preheating, place each chicken breast between 2 plastic wrap sheets and pound into ½-inch thickness with a meat mallet.
3. Evenly brush the mustard over each breast.
4. When preheating is complete, heat the ghee in the pot. Sauté the chicken, uncovered, for 3 minutes per side.
5. Stir in the salsa and lime juice and cook, uncovered for 5-6 minutes.
6. When cooking is complete, press START/STOP to end cooking. Sprinkle with the cilantro and serve warm.

Garlic Chicken

SERVES: 4

PREP TIME: 9 minutes
COOK TIME: 6 minutes

2 tbsps. ghee
2 tbsps. salted butter
1 pound (454 g) boneless chicken thighs, cut into 1-inch pieces
1 medium onion, cut into 1-inch pieces
1 medium carrot, roll-cut into ½-inch pieces
1 red bell pepper, cut into 1-inch pieces
½ cup whole-milk Greek yogurt
2 garlic cloves, crushed and chopped
1 tbsp. ginger, crushed and chopped
1 tsp. hot sesame oil
1 tsp. ground coriander
1 tsp. ground paprika
1 tsp. ground cumin
1 tsp. ground cloves

1. Turn dial to SEAR/SAUTÉ, set temperature to HI, and press START/STOP to begin preheating. Allow the unit to preheat for 5 minutes.
2. When preheating is complete, heat the ghee in the pot until it shimmers. Sauté the garlic, ginger, and carrot, uncovered, for about 1-2 minutes, stirring occasionally.
3. Add the chicken, onion, bell pepper, coriander, cumin, paprika and cloves to the pot. Cook for about 2-3 minutes.
4. Toss the butter and sesame oil and stir-fry for about 1 minute.
5. When cooking is complete, press START/STOP to end cooking. Stir in the yogurt and serve warm.

Caramelized Chicken Teriyaki

SERVES: 2

PREP TIME: 10 minutes
COOK TIME: 1 hour 40 minutes

1 tbsp. olive oil
2 chicken fillets
2 tbsps. Japanese Sake
2 tbsps. unsweetened soy sauce
1 tbsp. ginger juice
3 tsps. sugar
½ tsp. salt
white rice, for serving

1. Mix the ginger juice with salt and 1 tsp. sugar in a small bowl.
2. Rub the chicken with ginger mixture and leave it overnight to marinate.
3. Before getting started, add 12 cups of room-temperature water to the pot.
4. Cover with the lid and turn dial to SOUS VIDE, set temperature to 165°F and set time to 1 hour 30 minutes. Press START/STOP to begin preheating.
5. In the morning, carefully transfer the chicken into the Sous Vide bag.
6. When preheating is complete and "ADD FOOD" will show on the display.
7. Open the lid. Place the bag in water and seal it using the water displacement method. Close the lid.
8. When cooking is complete, remove the bag with chicken from the pot.
9. Pour off any remaining water and pat the pot dry with a paper towel. Turn dial to SEAR/SAUTÉ, set temperature to HI, and press START/STOP to begin preheating. Allow the unit to preheat for 5 minutes.
10. When preheating is complete, heat the olive oil in the pot. Place the chicken in the pot and sear both sides until light brown. Set aside.
11. Mix 2 tsps. sugar with sake and soy sauce in the pot. Boil until the sauce thickens a bit.
12. Pour half of the sauce over the cooked chicken fillets and torch the glaze until it caramelizes.
13. Chop the fillets and serve over white rice, drizzling with the remaining liquid half of the sauce.

Italian Chicken Marsala

SERVES: 2

PREP TIME: 10 minutes
COOK TIME: 2 hours 20 minutes

1 tbsp. olive oil
4 chicken breast fillets, bones and skin removed
1 pound porcini mushrooms, chopped
1 cup all-purpose flour
1 cup dry red wine
1 cup chicken broth
3 tbsps. freshly chopped parsley
Salt and pepper to taste

1. Before getting started, add 12 cups of room-temperature water to the pot.
2. Cover with the lid and turn dial to SOUS VIDE, set temperature to 165°F and set time to 2 hours. Press START/STOP to begin preheating.
3. Sprinkle the chicken breasts with salt and pepper and carefully put into the Sous Vide bag.
4. When preheating is complete and "ADD FOOD" will show on the display.
5. Open the lid. Place the bag in water and seal it using the water displacement method. Close the lid.
6. When cooking is complete, remove the bag with chicken breasts from the pot. Pat the chicken breasts dry with kitchen towels and dredge them in the flour.
7. Pour off any remaining water and pat the pot dry with a paper towel. Turn dial to SEAR/SAUTÉ, set temperature to HI, and press START/STOP to begin preheating. Allow the unit to preheat for 5 minutes.
8. When preheating is complete, heat olive oil in the pot. Place the fillets in the pot and brown until golden. Set aside.
9. Put the chopped mushrooms in the pot and sauté for about 5 minutes. Add the red wine and chicken broth, simmer for 10 minutes.
10. Pour the sauce over the chicken breasts and garnish with the freshly chopped parsley. Serve warm.

Panko Crusted Chicken

PREP TIME: 30 minutes
COOK TIME: 1 hour 40 minutes

4 boneless chicken breasts
1 lb. sliced mushrooms
2 eggs
1 cup panko bread crumbs
Small bunch of thyme
Salt and pepper
Canola oil

1. Before getting started, add 12 cups of room-temperature water to the pot.
2. Cover with the lid and turn dial to SOUS VIDE, set temperature to 165°F and set time to 1 hour 30 minutes. Press START/STOP to begin preheating.
3. Season the chicken with salt and thyme. Put the chicken breasts in a resealable bag.
4. When preheating is complete and "ADD FOOD" will show on the display.
5. Open the lid. Place the bag in water and seal it using the water displacement method. Close the lid.
6. When cooking is complete, remove the bag with chicken from the pot and pat dry.
7. Pour off any remaining water and pat the pot dry with a paper towel. Turn dial to SEAR/SAUTÉ, set temperature to HI, and press START/STOP to begin preheating. Allow the unit to preheat for 5 minutes.
8. Meanwhile, add the eggs into a container and dip the chicken in egg wash until well coated. Place the panko bread crumbs in a shallow container and add some salt and pepper. Put the chicken to bread crumbs and coat until well covered.
9. When preheating is complete, add the mushrooms in the pot. Cook until the water has evaporated.
10. Add 3-4 sprigs of thyme and stir well. Set aside.
11. Heat the oil in the pot. Fry the chicken for 1-2 minutes per side until golden brown. Serve with the mushrooms.

Ginger Spiced Chicken

PREP TIME: 20 minutes
COOK TIME: 7 hours

10 (4-ounce (113g)) boneless, skinless chicken thighs
3 onions, chopped
6 garlic cloves, minced
½ cup freshly squeezed orange juice
3 tbsps. grated fresh ginger root
2 tbsps. honey
1 tbsp. chili powder
1 tsp. ground red chili
½ tsp. ground cloves
¼ tsp. ground allspice

1. To treat the chicken thighs, use a knife to cut diagonal lines on the chicken thighs, so that the seasoning can better penetrate into the meat
2. In a small bowl, add the honey, ginger root, chili powder, chili powder, cloves and five-spice powder and mix well. Spread this seasoning evenly on the surface of the chicken, and set aside.
3. Place the onion and garlic in the pot, then top with the chicken. Pour in orange juice and cover with the lid.
4. Turn dial to SLOW COOK, set temperature to LOW, and set time to 7 hours. Press START/STOP to begin cooking, until the food thermometer shows 165°F.
5. When cooking is complete, remove the lid and serve immediately.

CHAPTER 7
NOODLES, PASTA AND SALAD

Cold Scallion Noodles

SERVES: 6 TO 8

PREP TIME: 10 minutes
COOK TIME: 15 minutes

2 tbsps. sesame oil, divided
6 ounces (170 g) whole-grain spaghetti
1 carrot, julienned
2 scallions, chopped
1-inch piece ginger, peeled and minced
2 tbsps. soy sauce
1 tbsp. rice vinegar
1 tbsp. sesame seeds
2 tsps. peanut butter
2 tsps. brown sugar or honey

1. Turn dial to SEAR/SAUTÉ, set temperature to HI, and press START/STOP to begin preheating. Allow the unit to preheat for 5 minutes.
2. When preheating is complete, carefully cook the spaghetti in the pot according to the package directions for al dente.
3. When cooking is complete, press START/STOP to end cooking.
4. Rinse the noodles with cold water and drizzle with 1 tbsp. of sesame oil to prevent the noodles from sticking.
5. Meanwhile, combine the remaining 1 tbsp. of sesame oil, vinegar, soy sauce, brown sugar, and peanut butter in a small bowl, mixing well.
6. Add the mixture over the noodles, then place the carrot, ginger, scallions, and sesame seeds, tossing to coat well.
7. Serve chilled.

Seafood Lo Mein with Pork

SERVES: 6

PREP TIME: 15 minutes
COOK TIME: 6 minutes

2 tbsps. cooking oil
1 pound (454 g) cooked noodles
¼ pound (113 g) ground pork
¼ pound (113 g) sea scallops, cut in half widthwise
¼ pound (113 g) medium shrimp, peeled, deveined, and cut in half lengthwise
1 medium onion, cut into 1-inch pieces
1 red bell pepper, cut into 1-inch pieces
¼ cup oyster sauce
2 garlic cloves, crushed and chopped
2 tbsps. rice wine
2 tbsps. soy sauce
1 tbsp. ginger, crushed and chopped

1. Turn dial to SEAR/SAUTÉ, set temperature to HI, and press START/STOP to begin preheating. Allow the unit to preheat for 5 minutes.
2. When preheating is complete, heat the cooking oil in the pot until it shimmers. Sauté the garlic, ginger, pork and onion, uncovered, for 2 minutes, stirring occasionally.
3. Add the bell pepper and shrimp to the pot and stir-fry for about 1 minute.
4. Put the scallops and stir-fry for about 30 seconds.
5. In a small bowl, whisk together the soy sauce, rice wine and oyster sauce. Pour the mixture to the pot. Toss in the noodles and cook for about 1 minute, stirring occasionally.
6. When cooking is complete, press START/STOP to end cooking. Serve hot.

Hakka Noodles with Pork and Cabbage

PREP TIME: 12 minutes
COOK TIME: 5 minutes

2 tbsps. cooking oil
1 pound (454 g) ground pork
1 pound (454 g) cooked noodles
1 medium onion, diced
1 medium carrot, julienned
1 cup shredded cabbage
2 garlic cloves, crushed and chopped
1 scallion, cut into ½-inch pieces
1 tbsp. ginger, crushed and chopped
1 tbsp. soy sauce
1 tbsp. fish sauce
1 tbsp. hoisin sauce
1 tsp. hot sesame oil
1 tsp. ground coriander

1. Turn dial to SEAR/SAUTÉ, set temperature to HI, and press START/STOP to begin preheating. Allow the unit to preheat for 5 minutes.
2. When preheating is complete, heat the cooking oil in the pot until it shimmers. Sauté the garlic, ginger and pork, uncovered, for 1 minute, stirring occasionally.
3. Add the onion, carrot and cabbage to the pot and stir-fry for 2 minutes.
4. Put the noodles and stir-fry for 1 minute.
5. Toss in the soy sauce, fish sauce, hoisin, coriander and sesame oil and cook for 1 minute.
6. When cooking is complete, press START/STOP to end cooking. Garnish with the scallion and serve warm.

Garlicky Carrot and Chicken Noodle Soup

PREP TIME: 10 minutes
COOK TIME: 8 hours

1 bone-in chicken breast, skin removed, about 8 to 12 ounces
1 cup diced carrots
1 cup diced celery
4 ounces (113 g) egg noodles
2 cups low-sodium chicken broth
3 garlic cloves, minced
1 sprig fresh thyme
1 tsp. red wine vinegar
⅛ tsp. sea salt
Freshly ground black pepper

1. Place the carrots, celery, chicken, thyme, garlic, broth, and salt in the pot. Gently stir to combine, then cover with the lid.
2. Turn dial to SLOW COOK, set temperature to LOW, and set time to 8 hours. Press START/STOP to begin cooking.
3. With 10 minutes remaining, discard the thyme and transfer the chicken on a cutting board. Add the egg noodles to the pot and continue to cook covered for 10 minutes, until the noodles are tender.
4. Meanwhile, shred the chicken with a fork. Discard the bone.
5. When cooking is complete, return the shredded chicken into the pot and stir in the vinegar. Season with the black pepper to taste. Serve hot.

Scallop, Mussel and Shrimp Pasta

SERVES: 8

PREP TIME: 15 minutes
COOK TIME: 3 hours

2 tbsps. butter, melted
1 lb. (454 g) medium shrimp, cooked and peeled
1 lb. (454 g) bay scallops, lightly cooked
1 pound (454 g) mussels, cleaned and debearded
3 cups linguine, cooked
4 cups shredded Monterey Jack cheese
3 cups sour cream
⅛ tsp. pepper

1. Add the butter, sour cream and cheese in the pot and mix well. Stir in the scallops, mussels, shrimp and pepper, then cover with the lid.
2. Turn dial to SLOW COOK, set temperature to LOW, and set time to 3 hours. Press START/STOP to begin cooking.
3. With 20 minutes remaining, discard any unopened mussels from the pot. Add the linguine and stir well. Cover the lid and continue to cook for 20 minutes.
4. When cooking is complete, garnish with fresh parsley and serve hot.

Steak with Arugula Salad

SERVES: 4

PREP TIME: 7 minutes
COOK TIME: 12 minutes

5 tbsps. extra virgin olive oil, plus 1 tsp.
8 cups loosely packed arugula, washed and dried
4 boneless strip steaks, 1 to 1¼ inches thick
3 ounces (85 g) Parmesan cheese, cut into thin shavings
2 garlic cloves, minced
1 tbsp. fresh-squeezed lemon juice
1 tbsp. chopped fresh oregano
1 tbsp. chopped fresh parsley
Pinch of salt
Fresh coarse ground black pepper

1. Turn dial to SEAR/SAUTÉ, set temperature to HI, and press START/STOP to begin preheating. Allow the unit to preheat for 5 minutes.
2. In a small bowl, whisk 5 tbsps. of olive oil with lemon juice, parsley, garlic, oregano and a pinch each of salt and pepper to taste.
3. Season the steaks strips with some salt and pepper.
4. When preheating is complete, heat 1 tsp. of oil in the pot. Sear the steaks strips, uncovered, for 6 minutes on each side.
5. When cooking is complete, press START/STOP to end cooking.
6. Spread the arugula leaves in 4 serving plates, then top with the steaks strips, lemon dressing and cheese. Serve immediately.

Egg Noodles with Scallions

PREP TIME: 5 minutes
COOK TIME: 15 minutes

2 tbsps. sesame oil, divided
½ pound (227 g) fresh Chinese egg noodles
6 scallions, thinly sliced
8 garlic cloves, finely minced
6 tbsps. unsalted butter
2 tbsps. light brown sugar
2 tbsps. oyster sauce
1 tbsp. light soy sauce
½ tsps. ground white pepper

1. Turn dial to SEAR/SAUTÉ, set temperature to HI, and press START/STOP to begin preheating. Allow the unit to preheat for 5 minutes.
2. Meanwhile, stir together the oyster sauce, brown sugar, light soy and white pepper in a small bowl. Set aside.
3. When preheating is complete, bring a pot of water to a boil and cook the egg noodles according to package directions. Reserve 1 cup of the boiling water, then drain. Drizzle 1 tbsp. of sesame oil over the noodles and toss to coat well. Set aside.
4. Pat the pot dry with paper towels. Turn dial to SEAR/SAUTÉ, set temperature to HI, and press START/STOP to begin preheating. Allow the unit to preheat for 5 minutes.
5. When preheating is complete, melt the butter in the pot until the foaming stops. Place the minced garlic and half the scallions in the pot and stir-fry for about 30 seconds, or until the garlic is softened.
6. Add the sauce and toss to combine well. Bring the sauce to a simmer and place the noodles. Stir the noodles to coat with sauce evenly. If the noodles need to loosen up a bit, pour in some of the cooking water, 1 tbsp. at a time. Continue to stir-fry the noodles for about 2 to 3 minutes, until they are heated completely.
7. When cooking is complete, press START/STOP to end cooking. Garnish with the remaining scallions. Serve warm.

Sesame Noodles with Peanut Butter

PREP TIME: 10 minutes
COOK TIME: 3 minutes

¼ cup peanut oil
¼ cup peanut butter
1 tbsp. hot sesame oil
1 pound (454 g) cooked noodles
4 scallions, cut into ½-inch pieces
2 garlic cloves, crushed and chopped
2 tbsps. cooking oil
2 tbsps. soy sauce
2 tbsps. powdered sugar
1 tbsp. sesame seeds
1 tbsp. ginger, crushed and chopped

1. Turn dial to SEAR/SAUTÉ, set temperature to HI, and press START/STOP to begin preheating. Allow the unit to preheat for 5 minutes.
2. Meanwhile, in a medium bowl, whisk together the peanut butter, peanut oil, sesame oil, powdered sugar and soy sauce until smooth. Set aside.
3. When preheating is complete, heat the cooking oil in the pot until it shimmers. Sauté the garlic, ginger and noodles, uncovered, for 1-2 minutes, stirring occasionally.
4. Pour the peanut butter mixture in the pot and toss for about 30 seconds.
5. When cooking is complete, press START/STOP to end cooking. Sprinkle with the scallions and sesame seeds and serve warm.

Turkey Sausage and Vegetable with Pasta

PREP TIME: 20 minutes COOK TIME: 5 hours	1 lb. (454 g) turkey sausage, cut in 1-inch chunks 1 lb. (454 g) pasta, cooked 14-oz. (397 g) can tomatoes, chopped 1 cup chopped green zucchini 1 cup chopped celery 1 cup chopped red onions 1 cup chopped green and/or red bell peppers 8-oz. (227 g) can tomato paste ¼ cup cooking wine 2 cups water 1 tbsp. Italian seasoning

1. Add all the in ingredients except the pasta the pot. Gently stir to combine, then cover with the lid.
2. Turn dial to SLOW COOK, set temperature to HI, and set time to 5 hours. Press START/STOP to begin cooking.
3. With 10 minutes remaining, add the pasta and stir well. Cover and continue to cook for 10 minutes.
4. When cooking is complete, remove the lid and serve immediately.

Spring Pasta Stew

PREP TIME: 20 minutes COOK TIME: 7 hours	6 large tomatoes, seeded and chopped 2 cups sliced button mushrooms 2 cups sliced cremini mushrooms 2 cups chopped yellow summer squash 2 red bell peppers, stemmed, seeded, and chopped 2 onions, chopped 1½ cups whole-wheat orzo pasta 8 cups roasted vegetable broth 5 garlic cloves, minced 2 tsps. dried Italian seasoning

1. Place the onions, garlic, mushrooms, squash, bell peppers, tomatoes, vegetable broth, and Italian seasonings in the pot. Gently stir to combine, then cover with the lid.
2. Turn dial to SLOW COOK, set temperature to LOW, and set time to 7 hours. Press START/STOP to begin cooking.
3. With 20 minutes remaining, add the pasta and stir well. Cover the lid and continue to cook for 20 minutes, until the pasta is soft.
4. When cooking is complete, remove the lid and serve immediately!

Seafood Salad

PREP TIME: 12 minutes COOK TIME: 3 minutes	2 tbsps. butter 2 cups iceberg lettuce, torn 1½ cups cooked lobster meat, chopped 1 tomato, chopped	½ of avocado, peeled, pitted and chopped ¼ cup feta cheese, crumbled 1 tsp. seafood seasoning

1. Turn dial to SEAR/SAUTÉ, set temperature to HI, and press START/STOP to begin preheating. Allow the unit to preheat for 5 minutes.
2. When preheating is complete, melt the butter in the pot. Sauté the lobster meat, uncovered, for about 2-3 minutes, stirring occasionally. Toss in the seafood seasoning.
3. When cooking is complete, press START/STOP to end cooking. Transfer the lobster meat to a large serving bowl. Put the remaining ingredients except the feta cheese and gently toss to coat well.
4. Top with the cheese and enjoy!

Beans, Sausage and Pasta Stew

SERVES: 8

PREP TIME: 30–35 minutes
COOK TIME: 4 hours

1 lb. (454 g) Italian sausage, casings removed
1 lb. (454 g) can kidney beans, rinsed and drained
26-oz. (728 g) jar meatless spaghetti sauce
1 medium yellow summer squash, cut in 1-inch pieces
2 medium carrots, cut in ¼-inch slices
1 medium red or green sweet pepper, diced
1½ cups spiral pasta, uncooked
1 cup frozen peas
⅓ cup chopped onions
4 cups water
1 tsp. sugar
½ tsp. salt
¼ tsp. pepper

1. Turn dial to SEAR/SAUTÉ, set temperature to HI, and press START/STOP to begin preheating. Allow the unit to preheat for 5 minutes.
2. When preheating is complete, add the sausage in the pot and sauté until no longer pin.
3. Drain and transfer into the pot. Add the kidney beans, squash, carrots, spaghetti sauce, pepper, onions and water to the pot. Stir to combine, then cover with the lid.
4. Turn dial to SLOW COOK, set temperature to HI, and set time to 4 hours.
5. With 20 minutes remaining, stir in the peas, pasta, sugar, salt and pepper. Cover the lid and continue to cook for 20 minutes, until the pasta is tender.
6. When cooking is complete, remove the lid and serve immediately.

Tuna and Beans Salad

SERVES: 8

PREP TIME: 10 minutes
COOK TIME: 5 minutes

6 tbsps. extra-virgin olive oil
¾ pound (340 g) green beans, trimmed and snapped in half
1 (12-ounce / 340-g) can solid white albacore tuna, drained
1 (16-ounce / 454-g) can Great Northern beans, drained and rinsed
1 (2¼-ounce / 64-g) can sliced black olives, drained
¼ medium red onion, thinly sliced
3 tbsps. lemon juice
1 tsp. dried oregano
½ tsp. finely grated lemon zest
Salt, to taste

1. Turn dial to SEAR/SAUTÉ, set temperature to HI, and press START/STOP to begin preheating. Allow the unit to preheat for 5 minutes.
2. When preheating is complete, add the green beans, ⅓ cup water and a large pinch of salt and bring to a boil in the pot. Cook the beans for about 5 minutes.
3. When cooking is complete, press START/STOP to end cooking.
4. Immediately transfer the green beans onto a paper towels lined cookie sheet and set aside to cool.
5. Mix together the tuna, Great Northern beans, olives and onion in a medium bowl.
6. Add the oil, lemon juice, oregano and lemon zest in another bowl and coat until well combined. Pour the dressing over the salad and slowly stir to combine.
7. Serve hot.

CHAPTER 8
SOUP AND STEW

Sweet Corn and Chicken Soup

SERVES: 6 TO 8

PREP TIME: 8 minutes
COOK TIME: 12 minutes

2 (14¾-ounce / 418-g) cans cream-style sweet corn
2 eggs, lightly beaten
2 cups cooked shredded chicken
8 cups chicken stock
1 scallion, chopped
3 tsps. cornstarch mixed with 2 tbsps. water (optional)
1 tsp. sesame oil
1 tsp. salt

1. Turn dial to SEAR/SAUTÉ, set temperature to HI, and press START/STOP to begin preheating. Allow the unit to preheat for 5 minutes.
2. When preheating is complete, add the corn to the chicken stock and bring to a boil in the pot.
3. Place the sesame oil, shredded chicken and salt. Return to a boil.
4. Stir in the cornstarch mixture (if using) to thicken the soup. Return to a boil.
5. Stir the soup with chopsticks and add the beaten eggs to the soup while stirring. Spin faster for a thinner, silky egg consistency; or slower for a thicker egg consistency.
6. When cooking is complete, press START/STOP to end cooking. Sprinkle with chopped scallion and serve hot.

Home-Style Curried Lamb Stew

SERVES: 6

PREP TIME: 15 minutes
COOK TIME: 3 hours 10 minutes

3 tbsps. extra-virgin olive oil, divided
1½ pounds (680 g) lamb shoulder chops
½ sweet onion, sliced
1 carrot, diced
3 cups coconut milk
1 cup beef broth
¼ cup curry powder
2 tsps. minced garlic
1 tbsp. grated fresh ginger
Freshly ground black pepper, for seasoning
Salt, for seasoning
2 tbsps. chopped cilantro, for garnish

1. Lightly grease the inside of the pot with 1 tbsp. olive oil.
2. Turn dial to SEAR/SAUTÉ, set temperature to HI, and press START/STOP to begin preheating. Allow the unit to preheat for 5 minutes.
3. Meanwhile, season the lamb with pepper and salt.
4. When preheating is complete, heat remaining 2 tbsps. of the olive oil in the pot. Brown the lamb, uncovered, for 7 minutes, stirring occasionally.
5. Add the carrot and onion to the pot and cook for 3 minutes, stirring occasionally.
6. Add the onion, coconut milk, curry, garlic and ginger to the pot. Stir to combine.
7. Place the lamb back into the pot. Nestle the lamb into the vegetables, then cover with the lid.
8. Turn dial to BRAISE, set time to 2 hours, and press START/STOP to resume cooking.
9. When cooking is complete, remove the lid and let cool for 5 minutes before serving.

Cajun Garbanzo Sausage Soup

SERVES: 7

PREP TIME: 20 minutes
COOK TIME: 3½ hours

2 cans (15 oz., 425 g each) garbanzo beans or chickpeas, rinsed and drained
1 can (14½ oz., 411 g) diced tomatoes, undrained
1 lb. (454 g) smoked kielbasa or Polish sausage, cut into 1-inch pieces
1 jar (16 oz., 448 g) mild salsa
2 celery ribs, chopped
1 medium onion, chopped
1 cup sliced fresh or frozen okra
3 cups water
2 tsps. Cajun seasoning

1. Add all the ingredients except the kielbasa in the pot. Gently stir to combine, then cover with the lid.
2. Turn dial to SLOW COOK, set temperature to HI, and set time to 3½ hours. Press START/STOP to begin cooking.
3. With 15 minutes remaining, add the kielbasa and stir well. Cover the lid and continue to cook for 15 minutes, until heated through.
4. When cooking is complete, remove the lid and serve immediately.

Fennel, Potato and Leek Soup

SERVES: 1

PREP TIME: 10 minutes
COOK TIME: 4 hours

1 fennel bulb, cored and chopped
1 white potato, peeled and diced
1 leek, white and pale green parts only, sliced thin
2 cups low-sodium chicken broth
2 tbsps. heavy cream
1 sprig fresh tarragon, roughly chopped (optional)
1 tsp. white wine vinegar or lemon juice
1 tsp. freshly ground fennel seed
⅛ tsp. sea salt

1. Place the fennel bulb, fennel seed, potato, leek, salt and broth in the pot. Gently stir to combine, then cover with the lid.
2. Turn dial to SLOW COOK, set temperature to HI, and set time to 4 hours. Press START/STOP to begin cooking.
3. When cooking is complete, stir in the vinegar to the pot and use an immersion blender to purée the soup. Add the heavy cream and stir well.
4. Top with fresh tarragon (if using) and serve hot.

Spinach Meatball Soup

SERVES: 10

PREP TIME: 15 minutes
COOK TIME: 3 hours

2 cans (14½ oz. 411 g each) Italian diced tomatoes, undrained
1 pkg. (24 oz., 672 g) frozen fully cooked Italian meatballs, thawed
1 carton (32 oz., 896 g) beef broth
4 cups fresh baby spinach (about 5 oz., 142 g)
2 celery ribs, sliced
3 medium carrots, sliced
1 small onion, chopped
2 cups water
¾ cup ditalini or other small pasta
¾ cup dry red wine or additional water
1 tsp. Italian seasoning
1 bay leaf
¼ tsp. pepper
Grated Parmesan cheese

1. Add all the ingredients except the ditalini, spinach and cheese in the pot. Gently stir to combine, then cover with the lid.
2. Turn dial to SLOW COOK, set temperature to HI, and set time to 3 hours. Press START/STOP to begin cooking.
3. With 15 minutes remaining, add the pasta and stir well. Cover with the lid and continue to cook for 15 minutes, until the pasta is tender.
4. When cooking is complete, discard the bay leaf. Add the spinach and stir until wilted. Serve hot with cheese.

Braised Beef and Potato Stew

SERVES: 8

PREP TIME: 20 minutes
COOK TIME: 4 hours 20 minutes

1 tbsp. olive oil
1 (3-pound, 1.4 kg) grass-fed chuck shoulder roast or tri-tip roast
8 Yukon Gold potatoes, cut into chunks
4 large carrots, peeled and cut into chunks
2 onions, chopped
1 leek, sliced
2 cups beef stock
8 garlic cloves, sliced
1 tsp. dried marjoram
½ tsp. salt
¼ tsp. freshly ground black pepper

1. Turn dial to SEAR/SAUTÉ, set temperature to HI, and press START/STOP to begin preheating. Allow the unit to preheat for 5 minutes.
2. While unit is preheating, season the beef with salt and pepper on both sides.
3. When preheating is complete, heat the oil in the pot. Place the beef in the pot and cook for 15 minutes.
4. After 15 minutes, use tongs to remove the beef from the pot and set aside.
5. Add the garlic, potatoes, carrots, onions and leek to the pot. Cook for 5 minutes, stirring frequently.
6. Add the beef stock and marjoram to the pot. Stir to combine.
7. Place the lamb into the pot. Nestle the lamb into the vegetables, then cover with the lid.
8. Turn dial to BRAISE, set time to 4 hours, and press START/STOP to resume cooking, until the beef is very tender.
9. When cooking is complete, remove the lid and serve beef with vegetables.

Ginger Egg Drop Soup

PREP TIME: 5 minutes
COOK TIME: 8 minutes

1 tsp. sesame oil
2 large eggs, lightly beaten
4 cups low-sodium chicken broth
2 scallions, thinly sliced, for garnish
2 peeled fresh ginger slices, each about the size of a quarter
2 garlic cloves, peeled
2 tbsps. cornstarch
3 tbsps. water
2 tsps. light soy sauce

1. Turn dial to SEAR/SAUTÉ, set temperature to HI, and press START/STOP to begin preheating. Allow the unit to preheat for 5 minutes.
2. When preheating is complete, combine the broth, garlic, ginger, and light soy and bring to a boil in the pot. Cook for about 4-5 minutes. Remove the ginger and garlic and discard.
3. In a small bowl, mix the cornstarch and water and combine well. Pour the mixture into the pot and stir for 30 seconds, until the soup thickens.
4. Dip a fork into the beaten eggs and then drag it through the soup, gently stirring as you go. Continue to dip the fork into the egg and drag it through the soup to make the egg threads. Once all the egg has been added, let the soup sit for a while to allow the eggs to set.
5. When cooking is complete, press START/STOP to end cooking. Drizzle in the sesame oil and ladle soup into bowls. Sprinkle with the scallions and serve hot.
6. After all the eggs have been added, let the soup sit for a while to allow the eggs to set. Drizzle with sesame oil and ladle soup into bowls. Sprinkle with scallions and serve.

Lotus Root and Pork Ribs with Goji Soup

PREP TIME: 10 minutes
COOK TIME: 4 hours

1 pound (454 g) lotus root, peeled and cut into ¼-inch-thick rounds
1 pound (454 g) pork ribs, cut into 1-inch pieces
12 cups water
½ cup dried red dates (optional)
¼ cup dried goji berries
2 tbsps. soy sauce
1 tsp. salt
½ tsp. peppercorns

1. Turn dial to SEAR/SAUTÉ, set temperature to HI, and press START/STOP to begin preheating. Allow the unit to preheat for 5 minutes.
2. When preheating is complete, add the pork ribs, lotus root, peppercorns, red dates (if using) and water in the pot. Cover to cook for at least 3 hours, or up to 4 hours.
3. When cooking is complete, press START/STOP to end cooking.
4. Add the soy sauce, salt and goji berries and let the soup rest for about 15 minutes for the goji berries to reconstitute, then serve warm.

Chinese Mushroom and Carrot Soup

SERVES: 6 TO 8

PREP TIME: 10 minutes
COOK TIME: 20 minutes

1 tbsp. olive oil
1 small bunch enoki mushrooms, roots removed
5 or 6 white or brown button mushrooms, cut into thin slices
4 or 5 large shiitake mushrooms, cut into thin slices
1 carrot, cut into thin slices
8 cups vegetable stock
¼ cup dried goji berries
½ onion, sliced
2 garlic cloves, minced
1 tbsp. soy sauce
2 tsps. sesame oil
1 tsp. salt

1. Turn dial to SEAR/SAUTÉ, set temperature to HI, and press START/STOP to begin preheating. Allow the unit to preheat for 5 minutes.
2. When preheating is complete, heat the olive oil in the pot. Sauté the onion and garlic until the onion become slightly translucent.
3. Add the carrot, button mushrooms, shiitake mushrooms, and enoki mushrooms to the pot and cook for 2 minutes.
4. Pour in the vegetable stock and bring to a boil. Place the sesame oil, goji berries, soy sauce and salt. Cook for about 15 minutes.
5. When cooking is complete, press START/STOP to end cooking. Let cool slightly and serve warm.

Carrot Chicken Noodle Soup

SERVES: 12

PREP TIME: 20 minutes
COOK TIME: 3½ hours

1¼ lbs. (568 g) boneless skinless chicken breast halves
1¼ lbs. (568 g) boneless skinless chicken thighs
4 cans (14 ½ oz. each, 411 g) chicken broth
1 pkg. (9 oz., 255 g) refrigerated linguine
12 fresh baby carrots, cut into ½-in. pieces
4 celery ribs, cut into ½-in. pieces
¾ cup finely chopped onion
2 garlic cloves, peeled and halved
1½ tsps. mustard seed
1 tbsp. minced fresh parsley
¼ tsp. cayenne pepper
½ tsp. pepper
Coarsely ground pepper and additional minced fresh parsley, optional

1. Add the celery, carrots, parsley, onion, cayenne pepper and pepper in the pot and combine together.
2. On a double thickness of cheesecloth, place the garlic and mustard seed; bring up corners of cloth and use kitchen string to tie to form a bag. Place the spice bag in the pot and add the broth and chicken. Then cover with the lid.
3. Turn dial to SLOW COOK, set temperature to HI, and set time to 3½ hours. Press START/STOP to begin cooking.
4. With 30 minutes remaining, discard spice bag. Remove the chicken and let cool slightly. Stir the linguine into soup, cover the lid and continue to cook for 30 minutes, until tender.
5. Meanwhile, cut the chicken into pieces.
6. When cooking is complete, place the chicken back to the pot and let it simmer in the soup for a few minutes. Sprinkle with coarsely ground pepper and additional parsley if desired.

Braised Lamb Stew with Carrots and Onions

SERVES: 6

PREP TIME: 15 minutes
COOK TIME: 3 hours 15 minutes

1 tbsp. olive oil
1 pound (454 g) lamb leg, trimmed of fat and cut into 1-inch pieces
4 large carrots, peeled and cut into 1-inch chunks
2 onions, sliced
2 leeks, chopped
1 cup fresh or frozen peas
3 cups (720 ml) beef broth
1 tbsp. dried rosemary
1 tsp. ground mustard
½ tsp. sea salt
¼ tsp. freshly ground black pepper

1. Turn dial to SEAR/SAUTÉ, set temperature to HI, and press START/STOP to begin preheating. Allow the unit to preheat for 5 minutes.
2. While unit is preheating, season the lamb with salt and pepper on both sides.
3. When preheating is complete, heat the oil in the pot. Place the lamb in the pot and brown for about 10 minutes.
4. After 10 minutes, use tongs to remove the lamb from the pot and set aside.
5. Add the carrots, leeks and onion to the pot. Cook for 5 minutes, stirring frequently.
6. Add the peas, beef broth, rosemary and mustard to the pot. Stir to combine.
7. Place the lamb into the pot. Nestle the lamb into the vegetables, then cover with the lid.
8. Turn dial to BRAISE, set time to 3 hours, and press START/STOP to resume cooking.
9. When cooking is complete, skim any excess fat from the surface of the stew and discard. Serve hot.

Beef Stew with Pumpkin and Tomato

SERVES: 6

PREP TIME: 15 minutes
COOK TIME: 4 hours

3 tbsps. extra-virgin olive oil
1 (2-pound, 907 g) beef chuck roast, cut into 1-inch chunks
1½ cups cubed pumpkin, cut into 1-inch chunks
1 cup diced tomatoes
2 cups beef broth
¼ cup apple cider vinegar
½ sweet onion, chopped
2 tsps. minced garlic
1 tsp. dried thyme
¼ tsp. freshly ground black pepper
½ tsp. salt
1 tbsp. chopped fresh parsley, for garnish

1. Turn dial to SEAR/SAUTÉ, set temperature to HI, and press START/STOP to begin preheating. Allow the unit to preheat for 5 minutes.
2. When preheating is complete, heat 3 tbsps. olive oil in the pot. Brown the beef uncovered for about 7 minutes.
3. After 7 minutes, stir in the tomatoes, broth, pumpkin, apple cider vinegar, onion, garlic, and thyme to the pot and combine well, then cover with the lid.
4. Turn dial to SLOW COOK, set temperature to HI, and set time to 4 hours, until the beef is very tender.
5. When cooking is complete, top with the parsley and serve.

CHAPTER 9
DESSERT

Blueberry Peach Cobbler

SERVES: 4 TO 6

PREP TIME: 15 minutes
COOK TIME: 2 hours

5 tbsps. coconut oil, divided
3 large peaches, peeled and sliced
2 cups frozen blueberries
1 cup rolled oats
1 cup almond flour
1 tbsp. maple syrup
1 tbsp. coconut sugar
½ tsp. vanilla extract
1 tsp. ground cinnamon
Pinch ground nutmeg

1. Use 1 tbsp. of coconut oil to coat the bottom of the pot.
2. Place the blueberries and peaches in the pot.
3. In a small bowl, add the remaining 4 tbsps. of coconut oil, oats, almond flour, coconut sugar, maple syrup, vanilla, cinnamon and nutmeg, and stir together until a coarse mixture forms. Top the crumbles over the fruits, then cover with the lid.
4. Turn dial to SLOW COOK, set temperature to HI, and set time to 2 hours. Press START/STOP to begin cooking.
5. When cooking is complete, serve immediately.

Brown Rice Pudding

SERVES: 6

PREP TIME: 10 minutes
COOK TIME: 8 hours

1 (13-ounce, 369 g) can light coconut milk
1½ cups (360 ml) skim milk
⅔ cup uncooked brown rice
½ cup dried fruit of your choice, such as raisins, cranberries, apples, or a mixture
¼ cup (60 ml) honey
1 tsp. ground cinnamon
1 tsp. pure vanilla extract
¼ tsp. ground nutmeg
Pinch sea salt

1. Place all the ingredients in the pot. Gently stir to combine, then cover with the lid.
2. Turn dial to SLOW COOK, set temperature to LOW, and set time to 8 hours. Press START/STOP to begin cooking.
3. When cooking is complete, remove the lid and serve immediately.

Cinnamon Sugar Pecans

PREP TIME: 15 minutes
COOK TIME: 4

1 tbsp. coconut oil
3 cups pecan halves
1 large egg white
¼ cup maple syrup
2 tbsps. ground cinnamon
2 tbsps. coconut sugar
2 tsps. vanilla extract
¼ tsp. sea salt

1. Lightly grease the inside of the pot with coconut oil.
2. In a medium bowl, add the egg white and whisk well. Then whisk in the vanilla extract, cinnamon, coconut sugar, maple syrup, and salt. Combine well.
3. Mix in the pecans and stir to coat well. Pour the pecans into the pot. Cover with the lid.
4. Turn dial to SLOW COOK, set temperature to LOW, and set time to 4 hours. Press START/STOP to begin cooking.
5. When cooking is complete, remove the pecans from the pot and spread them on a baking sheet. Let cool for 5 to 10 minutes before serving. Enjoy!

Pumpkin and Yogurt Bread

PREP TIME: 10 minutes
PROOF TIME: 60 minutes
COOK TIME: 15 minutes

cooking spray
2 large eggs
8 tbsps. pumpkin puree
6 tbsps. oats
6 tbsps. banana flour
4 tbsps. honey
4 tbsps. plain Greek yogurt
2 tbsps. vanilla essence
Pinch of ground nutmeg

1. Mix together all the ingredients except oats in a bowl and beat with the hand mixer until smooth.
2. Add the oats and mix until well combined.
3. Lightly spray the top of the mixture and the inside of the pot with cooking spray.
4. Place the mixture in the pot, then cover with the lid.
5. Turn dial to PROOF, set time to 60 minutes, and set temperature to 95°F. Press START/STOP to begin proofing.
6. While the dough is proofing, preheat conventional oven to 360°F.
7. When proofing is complete, remove the lid.
8. Place the entire pot (without the lid) in the conventional oven and bake for 15 minutes, until the bread is lightly golden.
9. When cooking is complete, remove the pot from the oven. Place onto a wire rack to cool and cut the bread into desired size slices to serve.

Peanut Butter Banana Bread

SERVES: 6

PREP TIME: 15 minutes
PROOF TIME: 60 minutes
COOK TIME: 40 minutes

cooking spray
1 cup plus 1 tbsp. all-purpose flour
1 large egg
2 medium ripe bananas, peeled
    and mashed
¾ cup walnuts, roughly chopped
⅓ cup granulated sugar

¼ cup canola oil
2 tbsps. creamy peanut butter
2 tbsps. sour cream
1¼ tsps. baking powder
1 tsp. vanilla extract
¼ tsp. salt

1. Mix together the flour, baking powder and salt in a small bowl.
2. Whisk together egg with canola oil, sugar, sour cream, peanut butter and vanilla extract in a bowl.
3. Stir in the bananas and beat until combined well. Then add the flour mixture and fold in the walnuts gently. Mix until well combined.
4. Lightly spray the top of the dough and the inside of the pot with cooking spray.
5. Place the dough in the pot, then cover with the lid.
6. Turn dial to PROOF, set time to 60 minutes, and set temperature to 95°F. Press START/STOP to begin proofing.
7. While the dough is proofing, preheat conventional oven to 330°F.
8. When proofing is complete, remove the lid. Use fingers to spread dough evenly across surface area of pot. Gently press fingers into dough multiple times to create dimples in the dough.
9. Place the entire pot (without the lid) in the conventional oven and bake for 40 minutes, until the bread is lightly golden.
10. When cooking is complete, remove the pot from the oven. Cut the bread into desired size slices and serve.

Apple Tart

SERVES: 2

PREP TIME: 15 minutes
COOK TIME: 25 minutes

1 tbsp. olive oil
3½-ounce flour
2½-ounce butter, chopped and divided
1 large apple, peeled, cored and cut into 12 wedges
1 egg yolk
1-ounce sugar

1. Lightly grease the pot with olive oil.
2. Mix half of the butter and flour in a bowl until a soft dough is formed.
3. Roll the dough into 4-inch round on a floured surface.
4. Add the remaining butter and sugar into the pot and arrange the apple wedges in a circular pattern.
5. Top with rolled dough and press gently along the edges of the pot. Then cover with the lid.
6. Turn dial to BAKE, set temperature to 390°F, set time to 25 minutes, and select START/STOP to continue cooking.
7. When cooking is complete, remove the lid and serve hot.

Apple Crisp with Oatmeal

SERVES: 6 TO 8

PREP TIME: 5 to 10 minutes COOK TIME: 3 hours	1 tbsp. olive oil 4 cups sliced, peeled apples ¾ cup quick oatmeal ⅔ cup sugar 1¼ cups water ½ cup brown sugar	¼ cup butter, at room temperature 3 tbsps. cornstarch ½ tsp. ground cinnamon ¼ tsp. ground allspice ½ cup flour

1. Lightly grease the inside of the pot with olive oil.
2. Place apples, water, sugar, cornstarch, cinnamon and allspice in the pot and mix well.
3. Mix the oatmeal, brown sugar, butter and flour in a small bowl until crumbly. Sprinkle on the apple filling. Cover with the lid.
4. Turn dial to SLOW COOK, set temperature to LOW, and set time to 3 hours. Press START/STOP to begin cooking.
5. When cooking is complete, remove the lid and serve warm.

Spiced Berry and Pumpkin Compote

SERVES: 10

PREP TIME: 10 minutes COOK TIME: 3 hours	1 tbsp. coconut oil 2 cups diced pumpkin 1 cup cranberries 1 cup blueberries 1 cup whipped cream ½ cup coconut milk ½ cup granulated erythritol Juice and zest of 1 orange 1 tsp. ground cinnamon ½ tsp. ground allspice ¼ tsp. ground nutmeg

1. Lightly grease the inside of the pot with coconut oil.
2. Add all the ingredients except the whipped cream in the pot. Gently stir to combine, then cover with the lid.
3. Turn dial to SLOW COOK, set temperature to LOW, and set time to 3 hours. Press START/STOP to begin cooking.
4. When cooking is complete, let the compote cool for 1 hour and top with a generous scoop of whipped cream, serve warm.

Easy Mac & Cheese

SERVES: 2

PREP TIME: 10 minutes COOK TIME: 10 minutes	½ tbsp. olive oil 1 cup cooked macaroni 1 cup grated Cheddar cheese ½ cup warm milk 1 tbsp. grated Parmesan cheese Salt and ground black pepper, to taste

1. Lightly grease the pot with olive oil.
2. Mix all the ingredients, except for Parmesan in the pot. Stir to combine, then cover with the lid.
3. Turn dial to BAKE, set temperature to 350°F, set time to 10 minutes, and select START/STOP to continue cooking.
4. When cooking is complete, top with the Parmesan cheese and serve.

Cream Bread

SERVES: 12

PREP TIME: 20 minutes
PROOF TIME: 60 minutes
COOK TIME: 55 minutes

cooking spray
4½ cups bread flour
1 large egg
1 cup milk
½ cup all-purpose flour
¾ cup whipping cream
¼ cup fine sugar
2 tbsps. milk powder
3 tsps. dry yeast
1 tsp. salt

1. Grease the pot lightly with cooking spray.
2. Mix together all the dry ingredients with the wet ingredients to form a dough.
3. Divide the dough into 2 equal-sized balls and roll each ball into a rectangle.
4. Roll each rectangle like a Swiss roll tightly and place the rolls into the prepared pot.
5. Lightly spray the top of the dough with cooking spray, then cover with the lid.
6. Turn dial to PROOF, set time to 60 minutes, and set temperature to 95°F. Press START/STOP to begin proofing.
7. While the dough is proofing, preheat conventional oven to 375°F.
8. When proofing is complete, remove the lid. Use fingers to spread dough evenly across surface area of pot. Gently press fingers into dough multiple times to create dimples in the dough.
9. Place the entire pot (without the lid) in the conventional oven and bake for 55 minutes.
10. When cooking is complete, remove the pot from the oven. Cut the bread roll into desired size slices and serve warm.

Sunflower Seeds Bread

SERVES: 4

PREP TIME: 15 minutes
PROOF TIME: 60 minutes
COOK TIME: 18 minutes

cooking spray
⅔ cup plain flour
⅔ cup whole wheat flour
1 cup lukewarm water
⅓ cup sunflower seeds
½ sachet instant yeast
1 tsp. salt

1. Mix together flours, sunflower seeds, yeast and salt in a bowl.
2. Add water slowly and knead for about 5 minutes until a dough is formed.
3. Lightly spray the top of the dough and the inside of the pot with cooking spray.
4. Place the dough in the pot, then cover with the lid.
5. Turn dial to PROOF, set time to 60 minutes, and set temperature to 95°F. Press START/STOP to begin proofing.
6. While the dough is proofing, preheat conventional oven to 390°F.
7. When proofing is complete, remove the lid. Use fingers to spread dough evenly across surface area of pot. Gently press fingers into dough multiple times to create dimples in the dough.
8. Place the entire pot (without the lid) in the conventional oven and bake for 18 minutes, until the bread is lightly golden.
9. When cooking is complete, remove the pot from the oven. Cut the bread into desired size slices. Enjoy!

APPENDIX 1:
BASIC KITCHEN CONVERSIONS & EQUIVALENTS

DRY MEASUREMENTS CONVERSION CHART

3 teaspoons = 1 tablespoon = 1/16 cup
6 teaspoons = 2 tablespoons = 1/8 cup
12 teaspoons = 4 tablespoons = ¼ cup
24 teaspoons = 8 tablespoons = ½ cup
36 teaspoons = 12 tablespoons = ¾ cup
48 teaspoons = 16 tablespoons = 1 cup

METRIC TO US COOKING CONVERSIONS

OVEN TEMPERATURES

120 °C = 250 °F
160 °C = 320 °F
180 °C = 350 °F
205 °C = 400 °F
220 °C = 425 °F

LIQUID MEASUREMENTS CONVERSION CHART

8 fluid ounces = 1 cup = ½ pint = ¼ quart
16 fluid ounces = 2 cups = 1 pint = ½ quart
32 fluid ounces = 4 cups = 2 pints = 1 quart = ¼ gallon
128 fluid ounces = 16 cups = 8 pints = 4 quarts = 1 gallon

BAKING IN GRAMS

1 cup flour = 140 grams
1 cup sugar = 150 grams
1 cup powdered sugar = 160 grams
1 cup heavy cream = 235 grams

VOLUME

1 milliliter = 1/5 teaspoon
5 ml = 1 teaspoon
15 ml = 1 tablespoon
240 ml = 1 cup or 8 fluid ounces
1 liter = 34 fluid ounces

WEIGHT

1 gram = .035 ounces
100 grams = 3.5 ounces
500 grams = 1.1 pounds
1 kilogram = 35 ounces

US TO METRIC COOKING CONVERSIONS

1/5 tsp = 1 ml
1 tsp = 5 ml
1 tbsp = 15 ml
1 fluid ounces = 30 ml
1 cup = 237 ml
1 pint (2 cups) = 473 ml
1 quart (4 cups) = .95 liter
1 gallon (16 cups) = 3.8 liters
1 oz = 28 grams
1 pound = 454 grams

BUTTER

1 cup butter = 2 sticks = 8 ounces = 230 grams = 16 tablespoons

WHAT DOES 1 CUP EQUAL

1 cup = 8 fluid ounces
1 cup = 16 tablespoons
1 cup = 48 teaspoons
1 cup = ½ pint
1 cup = ¼ quart
1 cup = 1/16 gallon
1 cup = 240 ml

BAKING PAN CONVERSIONS

9-inch round cake pan = 12 cups
10-inch tube pan =16 cups
10-inch bundt pan = 12 cups
9-inch springform pan = 10 cups
9 x 5 inch loaf pan = 8 cups
9-inch square pan = 8 cups

BAKING PAN CONVERSIONS

1 cup all-purpose flour = 4.5 oz
1 cup rolled oats = 3 oz
1 large egg = 1.7 oz
1 cup butter = 8 oz
1 cup milk = 8 oz
1 cup heavy cream = 8.4 oz
1 cup granulated sugar = 7.1 oz
1 cup packed brown sugar = 7.75 oz
1 cup vegetable oil = 7.7 oz
1 cup unsifted powdered sugar = 4.4 oz

APPENDIX 2:
NINJA FOODI POSSIBLECOOKER TIMETABLE

SLOW COOK CHART

TYPE OF MEAT	COOK TIME LOW	COOK TIME HIGH
BEEF		
Top or bottom round	8-10 hrs	4-5 hrs
Eye of the round	6-8 hrs	3-4 hrs
Chuck	8-10 hrs	4-5 hrs
Pot roast or brisket	7-9 hrs	3½-4½ hrs
Short ribs	7-9 hrs	3½-4½ hrs
Frozen meatballs	6-8 hrs	3-4 hrs
PORK		
Baby back or country ribs	7-9 hrs	3½-4½ hrs
Pork tenderloin	6-7 hrs	3-4 hrs
Pork loin or rib roast	7-9 hrs	3½-4½ hrs
Pork butt or shoulder	10-12 hrs	5-6 hrs
Ham, bone in (uncooked)	7-9 hrs	3½-4½ hrs
Ham (fully cooked)	5-7 hrs	2½-3½ hrs
POULTRY		
Boneless, skinless breast	6-7 hrs	3-4 hrs
Boneless, skinless thighs	6-7½ hrs	3-4½ hrs
Bone-in breast	6-7½ hrs	3-4½ hrs
Bone-in thighs	7-9 hrs	3½-4½ hrs
Whole chicken	7-9 hrs	3½-4½ hrs
Chicken wings	6-7 hrs	3-4 hrs
Turkey breast or thighs	7-9 hrs	3½-4½ hrs
FISH		
1-inch fillets	N/A	30-45 mins
OTHER		
Stew meat (beef, lamb, veal, rabbit)	7-9 hrs	3-4 hrs

VEGETABLE	PREPARATION	WATER	SEASONING	STEAMING TIME
Artichokes	whole	4 cups	olive oil, lemon zest	25-40 mins
Asparagus	whole spears	1 cup	olive oil	7-13 mins
Beans, green	whole	1 cup	garlic, minced	6-10 mins
Beans, wax	whole	1 cup	Italian seasoning	6-10 mins
Beets	whole, unpeeled	4 cups	garlic, minced	35-50 mins
Beet greens	coarsely chopped	1 cup	thyme	7-9 mins
Broccoli	trimmed stalks	1 cup	olive oil	1-5 mins
Broccoli	florets	1 cup	olive oil	5-7 mins
Brussels sprouts	whole, trimmed	1 cup	thyme	8-15 mins
Cabbage	cut in wedges	1 cup	lemon juice	6-10 mins
Carrots	¼ inch slices	1 cup	maple syrup	7-10 mins
Carrots, baby	whole	1 cup	honey and ginger	7-10 mins
Cauliflower	florets	1 cup	lemon juice	5-10 mins
Corn on the cob	whole, husks removed	2 cups	garlic butter	15-20 mins
Kale	trimmed	1 cup	olive oil and garlic	5-8 mins
Okra	whole, trimmed	1 cup	sautéed scallions	6-8 mins
Onions, pearl	whole	1 cup	lemon juice	8-12 mins
Parsnips	peeled, ½ inch slices	1 cup	Italian seasoning	7-10 mins
Peas, green	fresh or frozen shelled	1 cup	mint and lemon juice	2-4 mins
Peas, sugar snap	whole pods, trimmed	1 cup	mint and lemon juice	5-6 mins
Potatoes, all	½ inch slices	1 cup	parsley dill	8-12 mins
Potatoes, new	whole	4 cups	parsley or rosemary	15-20 mins
Potatoes, sweet	½ inch chunks	1 cup	honey	8-12 mins
Spinach	whole leaves	1 cup	olive oil	3-5 mins
Squash, butternut	peeled, ½ inch cubes	1 cup	maple syrup	7-10 mins
Turnips	½ inch slices	1 cup	Italian seasoning	8-12 mins
Turnip greens	coarsely chopped	1 cup	olive oil and garlic	4-8 mins
Swiss Chard	coarsely chopped	1 cup	olive oil and garlic	3-5 mins
Zucchini	1 inch slices	1 cup	olive oil and Italian seasoning	5-8 mins

SOUS VIDE CHART

INGREDIENT	AMOUNT	TEMP	TIME
BEEF			
Boneless ribeye	2 steaks, 14 oz each, 1-2 inches thick	125°F Rare 130°F Medium Rare 135°F Medium 145°F Medium Well 155°F Well Done	1-5 hrs
Boneless ribeye	3 steaks, 14 oz each, 1-2 inches thick		1-5 hrs
Porterhouse	2 steaks, 14 oz each, 1-2 inches thick		1-5 hrs
Filet mignon	4 steaks, 8 oz each, 1-2 inches thick		1-5 hrs
Flank	3 steaks, 12 oz each, 1-2 inches thick	125°F Rare 130°F Medium Rare 135°F Medium 145°F Medium Well 155°F Well Done	2-5 hrs
Flat iron	2 steaks, 10 oz each, 1-2 inches thick		2-5 hrs
PORK			
Boneless pork chops	5 chops, 6-8 oz each, 2½ inches thick	145°F	1-4 hrs
Bone-In pork chops	2 chops, 10-12 oz each, 2½ inches thick	145°F	1-4 hrs
Tenderloin	1 tenderloin, 1-1½ lbs, 2½ inches thick	145°F	1-4 hrs
Sausages	6 sausages, 2-3 oz each	165°F	2-5 hrs
Boneless pork shoulder	3 lbs, 3-4 inches thick	165°F	12-24 hrs
CHICKEN			
Chicken Breast	6 breasts, 6-8 oz each, 1-2 inches thick	165°F	1-3 hrs
Boneless Chicken Thighs	6 thighs, 4-6 oz each, 1-2 inches thick	165°F	1-3 hrs
Bone-In Chicken Thighs	4 thighs, 4-6 oz each, 1-2 inches thick	165°F	1½-4 hrs
Chicken Leg Quarters	2 quarters, 12-14 oz each, 1-2 inches thick	165°F	1½-4 hrs
Chicken Wings & Drummettes	2 lbs	165°F	1-3 hrs
Half Chicken	2½-3 lbs	165°F	2-3 hrs
SEAFOOD			
Whitefish (Cod, Haddock, Whiting, Pollock)	2 portions, 6-10 oz each, 1-2 inches thick	130°F	1-1½ hrs
Salmon	4 portions, 6-10 oz each, 1-2 inches thick	130°F	1-1½ hrs
Shrimp	2 lbs	130°F	30 mins-2 hrs
VEGETABLES			
Asparagus	1-2 lbs	180°F	30 mins
Broccoli	1-1½ lbs	180°F	30 mins
Brussels Sprouts	1-2 lbs	180°F	45 mins
Carrots	1-1½ lbs	180°F	45 mins
Cauliflower	1-1½ lbs	180°F	30 mins
Green Beans	1-1½ lbs	180°F	30 mins
Squash	1-1½ lbs	185°F	1 hr
Sweet Potatoes	1-1½ lbs	185°F	1 hr
Potatoes	1-2 lbs	190°F	1 hr

APPENDIX 3:
RECIPES INDEX

Made in the USA
Coppell, TX
13 October 2023

22787841R10044